Anyone Can Homeschool

by

Nicki Truesdell

Nicki Truesdell
Deuteronomy 6:6-9

Copyright © 2020 by Nicki Truesdell

All rights reserved. No portion of this book may be reproduced in any form without the written consent of the copyright owner, except for brief excerpts quoted in critical reviews.

First Edition

ISBN-10: 9798675326532

Dedication

To my husband, Randy, for giving me the idea to write this book, and encouraging me every step of the way.

To my mom, Debbie, who first showed me that anyone could homeschool.

Table of Contents

Introduction..1

Part 1

Chapter 1: Rethinking School............................9

Chapter 2: Teaching and Learning....................27

Chapter 3: Home Education on a Budget............43

Chapter 4: Special Needs................................55

Chapter 5: The Single Parent..........................73

Chapter 6: The "Unqualified" Parent..................91

Chapter 7: Chronic Illness in the Family...........103

Chapter 8: From Two Incomes to One...............115

Chapter 9: Dads, Grandparents, and

    Other Family Members...............................127

Chapter 10: The Only Child............................137

Part 2

Chapter 11: Getting Started.............................143

Chapter 12: Choosing a Curriculum..................153

Chapter 13: The Struggle is Real......................161

Chapter 14: The Law..169

Chapter 15: How to Get Started.......................179

Chapter 16: Encouragement for the Long Run....187

Introduction

In September of 2002, I suddenly became a single mom. I had two daughters, ages two and six, our clothes, and my car. I had about $200 to my name and no source of income. I was living in my parent's not-quite-finished new home. The future looked very bleak.

Besides my parents and a few close family members, everyone expected me to put my daughters in school and daycare, get a job, and live like everyone else.

We already had one year of homeschooling behind us, but that was in a comfortable home, and I had been a full-time stay-at-home mom. How in the world was homeschooling going to be possible now??

I was committed to homeschooling. I was not impressed with the direction public schools were heading. But even more, I didn't think that this sudden life change we were going through would get any easier for my little girls if they were also put in the care of strangers just weeks after moving out of the only home they'd ever known.

I was determined to keep our little family unit close together for the emotional health of my daughters. I had to find a way to earn money and still be a full-time mom, and also have an answer ready for all the naysayers.

That was in 2002. My daughters are now both graduates of home education and are well-adjusted, fully functioning adults.

So yes, I did find a way.

In fact, I found many ways. There were some rewarding times and some very difficult times. There were days and nights that I cried...a lot. We lived on a meager income many times. School subjects got delayed sometimes.

But when I look back over the years, I see the days and the hours that my children spent in the comfort and safety of home (wherever that was), and the gentle learning environment they grew up in. I remember days where they struggled emotionally from divorce, and I was there to comfort them.

I don't remember the stuff we couldn't afford to buy or the things we couldn't afford to do. I remember the moments with my children. And looking back, I know I wouldn't trade that for the world.

Anyone Can Homeschool

Yes, I do mean *anyone*.

You may be surprised by the title of this book. I know many people don't actually believe that *ANYONE* can homeschool. But I wouldn't say it if it weren't true. This book is the result of my own experiences, along with the stories of many friends of mine.

The first two chapters will introduce a way of thinking that you may not be familiar with if you're new to the idea of homeschooling. I will discuss what it means to teach and educate, and how children learn. I will open the door to a wider view of education: simply, that it doesn't all have to happen in a school building, and that it doesn't require a highly trained staff to accomplish.

The entire book depends on understanding these concepts.

Chapters 3-10 each address a specific concern for those who think they have no options. Feel free to jump to the chapter that addresses your need first. See the possibilities. Think outside the box. If you're like many, you may have a combination of issues. Maybe you're a single, working mom and your child has dyslexia. Maybe you're a working mom with little money for curriculum. I hope to help you see that the possibilities are there, and to point you to the resources you will need.

What I *won't* tell you is that this is a breeze. It's a commitment. It requires dedication. You will need to invest time, especially if money is not plentiful. You will become your child's principal, teacher, counselor, coach, and bus driver. You will be parenting on a *major* scale. You will have a new hobby and a new job.

And it will be worth every single minute.

I know this is possible because I have done it all. I was a homeschool student from 6-12th grade. That was in the 1980s before the explosion of homeschool curriculum vendors, co-ops, and the internet.

I attended a small, private school for my senior year and graduated with straight A's. I went on to college and received a Bachelors Degree in Business.

Did I forget to mention that my mom homeschooled me with a 9th grade high school education?

My own journey as a homeschooling mom has had its ups and downs, even after twenty years.

After my first marriage ended, I was financially broke, and had to start life over. I was unemployed, and then I worked part time. In order to continue homeschooling, I tried running my own business.

I remarried when my girls were seven and three. My new husband and I ran my business together, and it was not profitable. He took a part-time job on top of that, but we still struggled financially. There was *no* curriculum budget.

In the first year of our marriage, I was on pregnancy bedrest, then lost the baby at four months. Later that year, I got pregnant again, with more bedrest.

The next year, we sold our business and our house. We rented a house, and I took a part-time job waiting tables at night to help with finances. After a few months, I got pregnant again (yep, more bed rest). After six months in that house, we moved again.

We were in a new, smaller house (which was going to be very temporary!), now had four kids (including two little boys), and a small curriculum budget. Oh, and high school was approaching for my oldest daughter.

One more pregnancy (with bedrest). Now five kids in a 960 square foot home, aged newborn to fourteen. It was a *little bit crazy*.

Add in chronic migraines and you see a picture that no one would think conducive to homeschooling.

As you can see, my own homeschooling journey has given me the confidence to say that anyone can homeschool. It began with being taught by my own mom, who had no high school diploma, I have experienced divorce, single motherhood, working single motherhood, business ownership as a single working mother, remarriage, multiple pregnancies with bedrest, miscarriage, multiple moves, a small curriculum budget, no curriculum budget, working outside the home, multiple children of widely-ranging ages, a tiny house, and chronic migraines.

I am not a supermom.

There is no such thing. It is only that I made a choice to home educate and learned through each step of this journey that *there is a way*. Each stage had its challenges and its rewards, and our homeschool took on a different look each year.

And I'm not alone. My friend Lisa holds a part-time job and homeschools an only child with dyslexia. My friend Dianna is a single mom with four daughters. Tiffany works part time and homeschools her two children, one with special needs.

Through every stage of this journey, the one thing that gave me the confidence to keep going was my faith in God and my conviction that this was absolutely His will for my children.

As I mentioned earlier, I was a product of the early homeschooling movement that took root and grew through the 1980's. It was a distinctively Christian event. Though there were pockets of homeschoolers from a non-religious background, the current homechooling movement owes its growth to the Christian parents who removed their children from the public education system for religious reasons. The first handful of curriculum sellers and homeschool conventions were created and run by fundamental Christians. They were true pioneers. The homeschoolers of the 21st century stand on the shoulders of those first Christian parents.

So, while you do not have to homeschool for religious reasons, you will find that the majority of veterans, their advice, and the lessons learned are going to come from a Christian perspective.

This book will be no different.

If you have a desire to homeschool, I want to show you that there is a way. It will require your time, your flexibility, some research, and an investment of yourself, but it can be done.

I hope that this book inspires you to see the possibilities, the flexibility that home education allows, and to have the courage to step into the world of home education, no matter what your circumstances are right now. No matter *why* you want to homeschool, it is possible for everyone.

And since I believe the Bible's admonitions to parents include the full-time upbringing of their children, I pray you will rest in knowing that, when God calls you to do something, He absolutely provides a way to do it.

Charles Spurgeon, the great preacher of the 19th century, said, *"Home is the grandest of all institutions."*

Moms and dads, you have all that it takes to educate your children, whether your circumstances are ideal or not. You might hear from well-meaning family members that you can't do this. You might be told by school personnel that you're not qualified. You may be hearing from uninformed strangers that homeschooling just isn't for you.

But now I want you to hear it from people who are doing it, even in the most difficult of circumstances. You can do it. I did. They did. We still are. Where there's a will, there's a way. If you have picked up this book, you already have the will. Now let me show you the way.

Chapter 1:

Rethinking School

Educating a child is a natural process. Homeschooling is nothing more than an extension to parenting.

-Sue Maakestad

This is *the* most important chapter of this book, because in order to believe that anyone can homeschool, you may need to start thinking outside the "classroom" box. This is why I put it first. Without a complete shift in your thinking about education, you won't be able to see the enormous possibilities for each and every family.

THE CLASSROOM

When September comes around each year, many of us get a little giddy looking at the beautiful rows of crayons, new pencils, crisp white notebook paper, and fashionable backpacks at our local store. We feel a bit of sentiment when thinking about the first day of school, entering our new classroom on the first day and seeing the rows of clean desks, bright pictures on the wall, and a smiling teacher waiting to usher us into a new year of learning.

The public school classroom is a rite of passage for all of us. It's a familiar part of life that's hard to even consider letting go of. In fact, most of us can't even imagine not spending our entire childhood in a classroom.

And it's this classroom mindset that is the brick wall that stops so many parents from even considering home education. We assume we must recreate it at home and can't imagine accomplishing everything a school staff can accomplish.

Here's where we face this brick wall and smash it to pieces. Because homeschooling is not "school." It's not a miniature copy of the classroom.

Homeschooling is a very generic description of the parental act of providing an education outside the public school or private school. It does not have to look like the classroom you know (and probably grew up in). It *can* look like that, and for many homeschoolers, it often does. But the idea that *it must* is often the very thing that prevents many parents from giving homeschooling any consideration.

I want you to understand that it's just *one way* to homeschool. Replicating a public school classroom is a choice made by many parents. But it's not the only way to accomplish an education.

In fact, for many, it's not even the *best* way. And that's what this book is about. It's about what education looks like at home. It's about rethinking school. It's about rethinking education altogether. It's about parents taking the driver's seat in the education of their child and overseeing the timetable, the curriculum, and the method. It's about giving parents the confidence to see that they can provide the education their child needs, despite the seeming obstacles they face.

Home education is freedom. It's freedom to set your calendar, choose the curriculum, begin and end lessons on your own schedule, and decide what's working for your child. It's freedom to change up methods and materials when the need arises. It's freedom to be the parent, all the time. My friend Bethany, a former public school teacher and current homeschool mom says,

"The only thing I would do differently at the beginning would be to have not wasted all my time and energy trying to make it look like public school. I had the idea in my mind that we had to basically mimic public school. Our schedule was rigid, and we were miserable. The most liberty came in when I realized that the beauty of homeschool is making it look like what we needed for our home and not what the school puts into place to be able to teach twenty kids in one room."

Let me take a moment to blow your mind.

I'm going to tear some bricks from that wall...

- Did you know that some homeschoolers don't even think about grade levels?
- Did you know that many homeschoolers ignore the calendar and have school year-round, or all summer, or three days a week?
- Did you know that a typical homeschool day lasts about three or four hours, instead of seven or eight?
- Did you know that standardized tests are not at all standard among homeschoolers?
- Did you know you don't have to finish a textbook if it's not working out?
- Did you know that state history can be learned in 4th grade or 9th grade or whenever you choose to teach it?
- Did you know that grammar doesn't take twelve years to learn? Or math, or science, or history?
- Did you know that homeschoolers are taking preferred status in college admissions offices across the country?
- Did you know that homeschoolers have friends and social outings?
- Did you know that many activities in school classrooms are designed to be time fillers?

Don't try to imagine yourself running a miniature school, because that's not what you will be doing. You will be teaching your children the things they need to know, but on your own terms.

Sounds scandalous, doesn't it?

You see, in thousands of homes across America, there are children who sleep until 8:00 or even

9:00, eat a healthy breakfast without hurrying out the door, and begin school later in the morning. There are children who do, in fact, stay in their pajamas some days. There are children who watch their math lessons on the living room TV, lay on the floor to work their grammar lessons, and read a great book sprawled on their bed.

There are six-year-olds who spend no more than 1 hour per day on "schoolwork." There are high schoolers who work part time day jobs and do their schoolwork at night. There are single moms who school around their work schedule. There are kids who take most of their lessons online, and many who attend community classes each week. There are special needs kids who never use a pencil. And there are hundreds more variations of school happening in individual families everywhere.

The one thing that all these families have in common is that *they are learning*.

The individual learning and personalized schedules that are so common with home education are also what makes it successful. These parents have chosen to think outside the box; specifically, *the classroom box*. They have learned that you don't need a desk or a chalkboard or a bulletin board or a state lesson plan. What you do need is the willingness to find what works for your child.

And thanks to the boom in home education, whatever you do need for your child is probably already available.

You see, home educators have come to realize that learning is not only what happens when a child opens a textbook or sits in a classroom listening to a teacher lecture. In fact, it's often said that much more learning takes place outside the classroom where the natural curiosity of the child kicks in.

It's normal for us to see a classroom as the only means of education. Most of us today know one basic style of education: the public school. (Most private schools follow methods similar to public schools, although they have different funding and materials.) We know a few basic things about school:

- It's mandatory
- It takes twelve years of seven-hour-days
- It takes additional homework at night
- It takes certified teachers and a state-approved lesson plan

It's time for a bit more mind blowing here: none of those bullet points are true for home education.

You are not a school; you are a family. In the home, parents teach so many things. It comes naturally to us to teach our children how to walk and talk, tie their shoes, hold a spoon properly, and ride a bike. We let these things happen naturally, when the child is ready, instead of during the "school day" or the "school year." We don't use worksheets to teach table manners or give a quiz on the proper way to brush teeth.

We have all fallen for the notion that schools must teach everything, and a parent's job is reduced to feeding the children, clothing them, and shuttling them to their activities. It's no wonder that a large part of the population believes you must be certified to teach at all.

You may think it takes a 55-minute class to teach each subject each day, with a lecture, notes on a chalkboard, and follow-up worksheets. But you'd be wrong. It all depends on the child, the subject, and several other factors. My point is: *there is not just one way to teach.*

Parents are the Most Capable Teachers

Besides the fact that we are influenced by one main type of education, we are also trained to believe that only a *teacher* can teach. A large percentage of adults today are convinced that only a certified teacher could instruct a child in learning to read, doing math computations, understanding scientific discoveries, writing proper sentences, and remembering historic events.

Why are we so quick to doubt ourselves?

If you are not a certified teacher, you may not realize this about teacher certification: it's a degree that combines classroom management, child behavior, and teaching styles *along with* math, reading, writing, and science. Half of a teaching degree is the basic General Education requirement that any college student must receive. So you see, an engineering student or an accounting student will earn the same basic education credits (freshman and sophomore years) as an education major. The last two years of an education degree are a mix of philosophical training combined with varying degrees of education training.

For example, at the University of Oklahoma, a Bachelors Degree in Elementary Education only requires nine courses on the actual teaching of school subjects, like math, reading, social studies, science, etc. The rest of the courses are on child behavior, public speaking, communicating with parents, classroom culture, healthy lifestyles, etc.[1]

At the University of Cleveland, a Bachelors Degree in Middle School Education provides much more in the way of actual academic teaching; over twenty classes are offered for teaching specific subjects.[2]

I queried some of my teacher friends (who incidentally, now all homeschool their children) and they have verified this. Since education philosophy and preferred methods change with the winds (and the laws passed), the type of education a college graduate receives will depend on the year they graduated. A perfect example of this is how reading is taught: phonics vs. whole language.

This is not an attack on teachers. I am simply pointing out that if you are a parent, you are already a teacher. My goal with this book is to give parents the confidence to extend their parenting to the education of their own children by doing what they already do best: determining what's best for their child and finding a way to make it happen.

Education Training is Available to Everyone

As a homeschool veteran of over two decades, I can tell you that homeschooling parents have access to an amazing amount of education training in the form of workshops, seminars, and thousands of excellent books on the topic. I know I have put in enough hours of study to earn a master's degree myself, but I did it at home because I wanted to learn everything I could to be a great teacher to my children. There is no stopping a parent who is dedicated to helping their child succeed!

In addition, a good curriculum always includes a teacher's guide, with instructions on how to use that specific curriculum, teaching notes and dialog, and of course, the answers to the quizzes and tests. What's more, these curricula are usually published by small companies, and they have wonderful representatives available to help you when you (or your child) gets stumped, many of whom are just a phone call away. In many cases, the person answering the phone is the creator of the curriculum or an immediate family member. There are often accompanying websites and videos for the specific curriculum.

Couple this with the enormous amount of support groups available to homeschoolers, both locally and nationally, and you'll see how equipped even the most insecure parent can be to teach their own children. You never have to fumble blindly through your child's education.

The Myth of a Standard Education

One of the weaknesses of the classroom model is that it's narrowly focused on teaching one way, to one type of learner, at one moment in time. Classrooms contain up to thirty children in many cases, and a teacher must have an efficient method for managing that many students. In fact, it is *efficient classroom management* that has produced so much of what we think of as a normal part of education (and it makes up about 25% of an education degree).

Efficient management of classrooms includes a common curriculum with standardized methods of teaching and assessing results. Under this umbrella you will find the textbook, the worksheet, the grade-level system, the "discussion questions," the report card, and the state-mandated exam.

There is a lot of research on the different learning styles of children. Some children are those model students, who sit attentively at their desk each school day, raise their hand politely, know all the answers, and complete every homework assignment. According to Mariaemma Willis and Victoria Kindle Hodson, authors of *"Discover Your Child's Learning Style,"* this student is known as Perfect Paula.[3] She is the student that classrooms were designed for, and the student that college grads are trained to teach.

But that's not the only kind of student. As Hodson and Willis go on to illustrate, there are Wiggly Willy, Competent Carl, and Sociable Sue. Each of these children has their own personality that determines how they behave in a classroom setting. They are all unique and adorable, but they do not all learn in the same manner as Perfect Paula.

If you are a parent, you likely have one or more of these children. If you are a teacher, you've met them all! Everyone besides Perfect Paula struggles to follow the order necessary to keep a standard classroom full of children at a manageable level.

There are visual learners, auditory learners, and kinesthetic learners. Classrooms are generally geared toward a student who is mostly auditory. Children who need more visuals, or more hands-on activity or (gasp!) physical movement, are often left to struggle. Some of them get labeled and put into special programs. Some of them get into trouble. Some of them are medicated.

There are definitely great teachers who work hard to accommodate all types of learners, but the public school system is still part of the overall federal education system, and despite the fun activities a teacher provides, students must be able to read, remember, and regurgitate certain information on a standardized state test. With the enormous amount of expectations that public education teachers face, there is little opportunity for personalized learning to take place.

Now, I don't fault the teachers for this. Most teachers have a genuine desire to teach children. They love children and are passionate about education. But a taxpayer-funded system requires regular reports of progress, and this ties the hands of even the most dedicated teachers.

Let me encourage you: if you can read, write, and compute, you can teach it to your children. But that's not all. If you are not great at any of these subjects (or science or history or Spanish) you are still capable. Because you don't have to do it alone.

Homeschoolers have a secret weapon: homeschooling curriculum is a booming industry. I would venture to say that there are more curriculum options available to home educators than there are to public school children. There are traditional textbooks with teacher guides, non-traditional curricula, local group classes called "cooperatives," hybrid schools which mix group classes with home instruction, DVD lessons, and online classes. There's nothing you can't teach your child, even if you haven't mastered it yourself.

A whole new world

A beautiful thing happens when we start to look outside the classroom: children spend a smaller amount of time on schoolbooks and have more time to explore the wider world. That wider world may just be their own backyard, but they have more time and freedom to explore everything about the grass, the wildlife, the sky, the swing set, and the seasons. Maybe that wide world is just that: much wider than their own backyard. Maybe it's their community, the library full of books, running errands with Mom, working beside Dad, or traveling the country. Perhaps the wider world is found in classic literature, robotics, piano, acting, woodwork, or volleyball. The point is that less time is spent inside the four walls of a classroom and more time is spent in the real world.

And there are learning opportunities everywhere our children turn. The world is their classroom, and every person they meet is a potential educator. Every experience they have opens their mind to a new concept, hobby, idea, or story. They learn by seeing, hearing, and doing instead of just reading and regurgitating.

Learning happens with certain schoolbooks, yes. But it also happens in conversation, in trying, in listening, and in observing. Do you know how much natural science can be learned by being outdoors? A good stack of field guides and access to outdoor play can spark a variety of conversations and observations about the natural world and are far more interesting than a textbook or a worksheet.

Do you know how many beginning math concepts are learned through everyday life? Counting happens before preschoolers often know what numbers look like. Adding is a natural extension, though they can't hold a pencil to do a worksheet. Telling time happens by looking at an actual clock. Again, conversation, seeing, doing, and thinking are all very valid forms of learning.

This is why I stress that education is not just about a classroom and a stack of textbooks. Think outside the classroom. Knock down that mental brick wall.

Parenting 101

I often tell people that home education is a natural extension of parenting. When we have a baby, we anticipate every new achievement of that darling little child, from smiling, rolling over, and sitting upright to walking, talking, and playing with toys. But we don't just anticipate from a distance; we eagerly assist them in learning these things. We are their willing teachers in all things human.

And then a curious thing happens when a child turns five. Parents suddenly take off their teaching hats. They hang them up for occasional weekend use and turn that job over to the local school. They now believe that their child's education should be handled by professionals.

I am here to tell you that it is not only the professionals who can teach your child. As a parent, you have far more interest in your child's education than even the sweetest, best teacher at your local school. This is not an attack on teachers; this is honest truth about parenting.

A parent knows their child so instinctively in a way that the best teacher cannot hope to. A parent understands their child's emotional needs, strengths and weaknesses, and family circumstances. And a parent has the time that it takes to see and address these needs.

Certified teachers are necessary in public and private education. Since public schools are funded by our tax dollars, we absolutely want to be assured that the staff who is hired to teach our children has the credentials to do so. We would not want to hire unqualified people to be responsible for the education of the masses. It would be an inefficient and unwise use of education dollars. Private schools are directly funded by the parents of the students for the most part, so these parents also want the assurance that their school is staffed by qualified teachers.

This is true with any situation. If you pay for piano lessons, gymnastics, or math tutoring, you want to be sure that the instructors are well-qualified to teach.

Further, I know that teachers choose their profession because they love it. They genuinely want to teach children and want to make a difference. The world needs teachers. The majority of our population relies on the public schools.

But this does not mean that it's the only way to educate children, and it does not mean that a parent is not qualified or capable to teach their own. You don't need a license or degree to teach your children the things that they learn *before* kindergarten. And I can say with certainty and experience that you don't need a degree to teach them the things they learn during formal school years.

With confidence, support, and a great stack of books, any parent can be their child's teacher. The parent who didn't graduate high school, the parent who can't remember their algebra, the parent who works full time, the parent who feels they can't afford it, the parent with disabled children, and even the grandparent who is raising their grandkids --- they can absolutely do it. YOU can do it.

Is that brick wall coming down yet?

Let's take a look at the types of families, and family situations, on the other side of that brick wall:

- Single parents
- Working parents
- Self-employed parents
- Traveling families
- Special needs kids
- Low-income families
- "Uneducated" parents
- Parents with one child
- Large families
- Grandparents
- Families with chronic illness

And behind that brick wall you'll find that education takes on many forms:

- Traditional textbooks at home
- Whole-book style learning
- Hands-on learning
- Cooperative community classes
- Integrated classes and home study
- Online classes
- DVD programs
- Paid tutors
- Eclectic mixes of all the above

You'll find even more variations on these styles behind that brick wall that involve calendars, schedules, and grade levels:

- Year-round schooling
- Strict school-year calendar schooling
- 4-day school
- RV schooling
- Unschooling

Now that you have seen many of the possible ways for a child to learn, you will understand why I am bold enough to claim that *anyone* can homeschool. -Susan Schaeffer Macaulay, in her book *For the Children's Sake*, reminds us that anyone can do this because it's about relationships, time, and so much more than a school room:

"There has never been a generation when children have so desperately needed their parents' time, thoughtful creativity, and friendship. The surrounding culture is deeply out of step with the Word of God. Other pressures threaten to take away sanity, stability, and simple humanity.

One of the greatest powers for good is a family whose members respect each other and who have learned to function, however poorly, with the rich concepts the Word of God gives us as human beings. It is almost incredible to think of the stabilizing effect ordinary families can have not only for themselves, but as a light in a troubled generation."

Chapter 2:

Teaching and Learning

Once I realized we didn't need to recreate the traditional classroom, and that we could customize our kids' education, I discovered a new type of freedom.

— Kent Larson, 12 Homeschool Myths Debunked: The Book for Skeptical Dads

You may be thinking, "I have no idea how to teach school subjects. I can't begin to imagine how to teach a child to read." I think every homeschool parent has had that very same thought at one point or another. After all, we've been conditioned to believe that only a college graduate with a teaching certificate could educate children. Feeling inadequate is one of the top two reasons that most parents don't think they can homeschool (and money is the other).

But "educated experts" are a fairly new idea, as far as the history of the world is concerned. Before the 20th century, teachers came in many forms: parents, tutors, clergy, teenage girls, matronly older women, and private-school professors. Throughout the world and throughout time, education has been accomplished in so many forms it would take a separate book to compile them all.

But despite that, and despite the lack of modern college degrees, the human race has progressed through the centuries with new ideas, new inventions, exploration, the spread of information, and advances in science. Before modern education, men could measure and map the earth, view and count the stars and planets, translate languages, compile histories, and create nations. Don't think for a moment that our ancestors were "cavemen." I would go so far as to claim that many of them were much more educated than we are today. Our modern method of education is just one more method in a long series of different forms.

As I mentioned in Chapter 1, we hire certified teachers in our school system because they are taxpayer funded. If I wanted to hire a private tutor to come to my home, I could decide if the degree and certification were important to me, because I'm the only one paying, and my family is the only one who benefits.

Home education is similar. You are a private entity. You can choose how your child receives their education. And *you* can provide that entire education, college degree or not.

But how do you know what to teach? When to teach it? When they've mastered it? When to move them ahead? Isn't this complicated?

It's not. We are so blessed to live in the 21st century when so much information is available at your fingertips. This includes how to teach, how children learn, and different styles of homeschooling. I'll break these down into manageable bits of info, and there is more to discover on my website.

Learning Styles

This is a fascinating subject. If you've ever taken a personality test, you'll enjoy this. Each of us has a learning style, usually closely related to our personality traits. There are roughly four styles, or modalities, and your child will have at least 1 dominate one. That doesn't mean they don't have the other four; it just means that one learning style or preference stands out from the rest.

These 4 basic styles were categorized by Neil D. Fleming, which are known as the VARK model.[4] The acronym VARK stands for Visual, Aural, Read/write, and Kinesthetic sensory modalities that are used for learning information.

Visual Preference- Students who have a visual strength or preference:

- want the teacher to provide demonstrations
- find it easy to learn through descriptions
- often use lists to keep up and organize thoughts

- often recognize words by sight
- often remember faces but forget names
- often have well developed imaginations
- are easily distracted by movement or action in the classroom
- tend to be unaware of noise
- Roughly 60% of students are visual learners.

Auditory Preference - Students who have an auditory strength or preference:

- want the teacher to provide verbal instructions
- find it easy to learn by listening
- enjoy dialogues, discussions, and plays
- often remember names but forget faces
- often do well working out solutions or problems by talking them out
- are easily distracted by noise and often need to work where it is relatively quiet
- often do best using recorded books

Tactile Preference - Students who have a tactile strength or preference:

- do best when they take notes either during a lecture or when reading something new or difficult
- often like to draw or doodle to remember
- do well with hands-on activities such as projects, demonstrations, or labs

Kinesthetic Preference - Students who have a kinesthetic strength or preference:

- do best when they are involved or active
- often have high energy levels
- think and learn best while moving
- often lose much of what is said during lecture
- have problems concentrating when asked to sit and read
- prefer to do rather than watch or listen
- Most children are kinesthetic and become more tactile in the first grade[5]

If you're like most parents, you probably spotted yourself in one of these categories, and quite possibly your child or children, as well. Again, everyone has a mix of these, but there is usually one that's more dominant than the rest.

We will typically want to teach in the way that we, as parents, learn best. But if we want our children to get the most out of a concept, it's smart to find resources that fit their learning style. There are some wonderful resources available that go much further into the 4 modalities, and the homeschool curriculum industry has an excellent variety of resources that are tailored to the different learning styles.

So, if you have a child that needs to move, or see, or do, you're not tied down to the traditional lecture/textbook/worksheet method that public schools specialize in. As a homeschool parent, you have the flexibility to create a learning environment where your child absorbs information like a sponge, and even better, he or she is excited about it!

I have provided a link on *AnyoneCanHomeschool.net* for up-to-date information on VARK, articles on teaching to the different modalities, and learning resources for every type of learner. Maybe you're already aware of your child's learning style. If not, you will learn it with the daily observation that homeschooling affords.

Just remember, learning styles are helpful when preparing to teach your children, but they do not have to be your master. You may end up choosing a curriculum that wouldn't appear to suit your son's learning style, but you can certainly adapt it.

If he's a Wiggly Willy and hands-on learner, and you feel comfortable with a traditional textbook approach, there's a happy medium: use your textbooks and allow him to sit where he's comfy, give him permission to answer spelling tests verbally, or to write in his textbook with colored pencils. Even if you're working within a well-structured box, you can certainly think outside that box here and there.

Homeschooling Styles

Traditional – This is school as most of us know it: textbooks, worksheets, tests, and grades. It's familiar and comfortable and is what many first-time homeschoolers do first. There are several well-known publishers in the traditional homeschooling category. You can order a complete grade-level kit (including teacher guides, textbooks, workbooks, answer keys, and usually even additional resources, like science experiment supplies), or you can pick and choose the subjects and resources you'd like to focus on.

Classical - Laura Berquist, in *Classical Education and How to Implement it in a Large Family*, explains:

Classical education is the education that all educated people in western civilization once received, and it is an education that is ordered to teaching men how to think well about the highest and noblest objects.[6]

The classical model breaks learning down into three stages, completed over the 12 years of a child's education: the Grammar stage, the Logic stage, and the Rhetoric stage. In the Grammar stage, children memorize many things, including math facts, parts of speech, important history dates, etc. Children in the Logic stage are now utilizing the information they have memorized and beginning to think critically (while exploring the Grammar stage concepts on a deeper level). The Rhetoric stage (typically high school) involves an even deeper exploration of the same concepts with the practice of debate, writing, and persuasive conversation.

The study of Latin (and often Greek) is a mainstay of classical education. Students learn world history and scientific history and discoveries on a 4-year timeline that repeats three times over the course of their schooling.

Of course, in a homeschool setting, there are many variations, and plenty of books and curricula for parents who would like to give their students a classical education at home. It may sound daunting, but with the enormous help and resources available, it's not. It's a beautiful way to learn.

Charlotte Mason (or CM) – From *Ambleside Online*:

Charlotte Mason was a British educator who believed that education was about more than training for a job, passing an exam, or getting into the right college. She said education was an atmosphere, a discipline, and a life; it was about finding out who we were and how we fit into the world of human beings and into the universe God created. Charlotte Mason believed that children are able to deal with ideas and knowledge, that they are not blank slates or empty sacks to be filled with information. She thought children should do the work of dealing with ideas and knowledge, rather than the teacher acting as a middleman, dispensing filtered knowledge. A Charlotte Mason education includes first-hand exposure to great and noble ideas through books in each school subject, and through art, music and poetry.[7]

It's a beautifully gentle way of learning. I really think it's perfect for kids who have previously been in a traditional school setting but did not thrive there, for whatever reason. It does not involve rigorous testing or deadlines, but instead gives children access to the wide world and encourages them to learn through every experience.

Unit Study – From Amanda Bennet, a leader in unit studies:

I am often asked to explain what a unit study is, usually by newcomers to homeschooling or frustrated textbook parents. Well, first let me tell you what it is not. A good unit study does not involve dry reading or memorization, busy work, endless worksheet completion, and bored children.

A good unit study involves learning about one topic in an interesting and engaging way that will captivate the student and make them want to learn more and continue to think about the things they are learning. From cell phones to Ethiopia to catapults and elephants, unit studies can open the world to your child, one topic at a time.[8]

Unit studies are actually one of my first recommendations for new homeschooling parents. Pick an interest, any interest, and let your child explore it by following every rabbit trail they like. Take horses, for example. A unit study on horses would involve breeds, uses, the history of horses in America, the science of horse movement, the science of speed, racehorses, cowboys and ranchers, farm life, and so much more. This is education freedom at its finest!

Unschooling- This is a very generic term for allowing education in the home to be student-led. It does not mean "not schooling;" it simply means that the education looks nothing like a traditional school or any of its methods. The parent gives their child the tools to learn and allows them to follow their interests.

Depending on who you talk to, unschooling has many different levels. Some parents allow child-led learning for most subjects, but still have structured math lessons. Other parents allow their child to naturally learn all subjects on their own timeframe.

Whole Book Learning (also known as "living books") – This is pretty much like it sounds: reading books to learn. This is the method our family uses. Instead of a stack of textbooks for each subject, we use great books to dive deeply and learn about our topics, including history, geography, science, literature, art, and music.

What does that look like? For us, it means following a timeline of events and exploring the people and places involved through historical fiction, non-fiction, maps, art, and original writings. If we're studying the gold rush of 1849, we will read a good historic fiction about it, pull out maps and see where the first gold discovery in California happened. If we can find books that feature diaries or journals of people involved, we definitely read those. We will read about the different methods of mining gold, like panning in streams or mining underground. For art or music, we might search out some of the songs the miners would sing around a campfire. To explore the culture, we'll talk about

Levi's jeans, boom towns, and sample recipes that miners ate.

It's kind of like a bunch of mini-unit studies all connected together. But the main resource we use is good books. Lots and lots of good books.

Whole-Book Learning has a bit of crossover with Charlotte Mason style and Classical style homeschooling, because they also tend to use "living books" for learning.

Computer/Internet – This is quickly becoming one of the most popular ways to educate at home, thanks to modern technology. A few years ago, computer-based curriculum came in the form of CD-ROM, but many of those are transitioning to online learning, and new options spring up constantly. They range from single-subject classes to complete curricula and serve all ages, budgets, and schedules.

Some online courses involve live or recorded video, while others are more of a guided list of assignments. The flexibility within the computerized curriculum world is endless!

Eclectic – This is an easy way to say, "we use a mix of several styles and curricula." After a couple of years, many parents find this is their favorite. Choosing a math curriculum from one company, history from another, and taking English courses online is exactly what "eclectic homeschooling" is.

And this is just where my family is. After 20 years of homeschooling, I've found the things we like, but I'm also willing to experiment with something new or different when the need arises. That's "eclectic."

Teaching

This may all seem daunting, but don't forget that you've been a teacher since your first child was born. You've taught them all the things they need to know, up through kindergarten. You can continue teaching them. But now, there are answer keys and instructor guides!

Yes! Any good curriculum is going to include a teacher's guide of some sort. Some are extremely comprehensive, and others offer a basic "how to." There are numerous books and websites devoted to teaching specific subjects. And there's a constantly updated list on my website just for you.

Please rest assured that you already know so much of what your students will learn, especially in the elementary years. However, even the high school years aren't as scary as they sound. I have really enjoyed teaching my high schoolers, and I have made great use of the instructor guides, answer keys, and internet searches available to help me when I am stumped. I mean, how many of us remember what a present participle is, anyway? But about fifteen seconds of internet searching, and the reminder is right there in front of you.

For example, math has never been my strength. I didn't like it in school, and it's my least favorite subject to teach (especially in high school). It's not impossible, so we make it work. But often there is a problem or a question that arises that even the teacher book doesn't clear up for me. So, I consult the internet. I've found quick and clear answers on YouTube and in Google searches. And sometimes, believe it or not, if I don't understand the answer we've found online, my child still does.

So, relax.

You see, you don't need to be proficient in every single school subject. You just need to be willing to find answers you don't know and ask for help when you need it. Thanks to the internet, some great explanations are available in the form of text, video, and demonstrations for every subject you will encounter: dissections for biology, algebraic equations, advanced grammar concepts, and how the electoral college works. You'll find all you need to know about compiling a high school transcript, preparing for SATs and college, and how to earn scholarships. Visit *AnyoneCanHomeschool.net* for links to these resources.

Because homeschooling has exploded in growth over the last thirty years, there is an ever-expanding library of great books that inform, encourage, and train. You do not have to do this blindly, no matter your background.

As you're teaching your children, you're also going to teach them *how to learn*. This is such a valuable gift, and one that will serve them well throughout their lives. Show them how to study, explore, and find answers to their questions and you will change their world forever.

Graduation

This is a confusing and misunderstood topic for those not familiar with home education, so let me put your mind at ease. Many people still believe that a homeschooler doesn't get a real diploma or really graduate. Oh, but they do!

What is a diploma?

A diploma is simply a certificate stating that a person has completed a required course of study. When a homeschooled child completes the requirements set by their parents (or in some cases, their state), they are eligible to receive a diploma. It is proof of completion. In my home state of Texas, parents may order a diploma from one of several companies that produce them, and the parent will present it to their student. Other states in the U.S. have different requirements for graduation. Though most don't set out specifics, you should check with your state homeschooling organization to know the laws before you begin.

What is a graduation?

It's simply a ceremony that celebrates the completion of an education. It's a public declaration. And homeschoolers hold graduation ceremonies every year, in many different forms. Some look like any other school's graduation ceremony, with caps, gowns, and speeches. Others choose a private party in their homes or with a small group of friends. In our family, my two oldest daughters have participated in a traditional ceremony as part of our local homeschool support group.

At the end of their schooling, homeschool graduates are as legitimate as all other graduates. They enter college, join the military, and enter the work force with great acceptance. More and more, universities and companies *seek out* homeschool graduates.

Now that you have the information you need to understand teaching and learning, you're ready to see how these apply to your current living situation. No matter what circumstances you have (or how many obstacles you may face) home education is a completely viable option for ANYONE, including you!

CHAPTER 3: HOME EDUCATION ON A BUDGET

Most people think you have to give up so much to homeschool...in reality, you gain so much more!

– Karen DeBeus

The number one objection to the feasibility of homeschooling is cost. Whether it's a parent desperate for an alternative to public school, or a random stranger who comments that "it's just not possible for everyone," this belief is at the top of the list.

It's easy to see why! The amount that the government spends on public education, as well as the high cost of private school tuition, would naturally cause parents to assume that one must spend a great deal to educate children.

The reality is quite the opposite.

The amount of money required to provide an excellent education is very small. Do parents spend hundreds of dollars each year on homeschool curriculum and activities? Yes, some do. Is it necessary? Usually not.

In our family, the most we ever spent for a year of curriculum was about $200. Many years it's been much less, and some years it's close to zero. Over time, we accumulate a lot of reusable materials (like math books, for instance) so the cost of educating younger siblings actually goes *down*.

Sometimes I've needed a large stack of curriculum, and other times I've needed to be resourceful due to changing circumstances.

As an example, let me tell you how I taught my daughter to read without spending more than a few dollars.

When my 2nd child was about seven years old, I began formally teaching her to read. Life circumstances, such as two pregnancies with bedrest and two moves, all in two years, had dictated our schedule. And you know? This is one of the *benefits* of homeschooling, *not* one of the roadblocks. Life circumstances happen to everyone, but the beauty of homeschooling is that you can be flexible.

So, when life was eventually back to some sort of normalcy, I was ready to buckle down and teach her to read. There was one problem: our budget didn't have any extra for curriculum. So how did we accomplish it? Determination and some research.

Most parents think that they need an elaborate program that costs hundreds of dollars to teach reading. Not necessarily.

First, I found a used copy of the A Beka *Handbook for Reading* around $3. That book is laid out so perfectly and easily. I didn't have the teacher's guide, but I didn't need it. My daughter and I read one new sound (one page) in the book each day. The next day, we'd review all the previous sounds, and add a new one. Within a couple of weeks, she was sounding out simple words. We went pretty far in the Handbook with this simple method but didn't finish because she just didn't need to.

Because she was a "worksheet" kind of girl, I found some free resources online. With a simple internet search, I found handwriting pages and phonics worksheets to supplement her work. I simply based my search on what she was learning (for example "free printable long-E worksheets"). One or two worksheets per concept usually sufficed, but I could easily adjust this for her needs. I also looked up lists of basic sight words for her to practice. I actually let her read these on the computer screen.

Once she could read on a basic level, we used two resources for practice: free online books and the library. Our local library was small, and we quickly went through all of their easy readers. Internet to the rescue! Project Gutenberg is a website devoted to free online books in the public domain. I quickly found many vintage, easy readers for her to practice with each day.

We spent about 15-30 minutes per day on these various exercises. Within the year, she was an independent reader. She quickly fell in love with the Magic Tree House books, and then moved on to other series. By age 10 she was an avid reader, and at 12-13, she was reading and enjoying classics. She is now a high school graduate and reads classic literature, like *Dante's Inferno* and *The Man in the Iron Mask* for enjoyment.

This story is just one example of how I have personally managed to teach a child without a curriculum budget. It doesn't take a superpower; it just takes determination and a bit of your free time. Disclaimer: You'll probably notice that a smaller budget could require more of your time due to internet searches and scouring used curriculum sales. Let me tell you, it is worth it.

You know the old saying, "Where there's a will, there's a way"? It is absolutely true.

Moms and dads, can you think of areas of your parenting where you faced an obstacle and forged ahead, no matter what? You can do this with education, too!

After years of applying this method at various times, I am convinced that it is applicable to any subject at any age. We live in the information age. It's a great time to be a homeschooler!

Back to basics

When encouraging parents in beginning their homeschool journey, I ask them to consider what is really necessary for a basic education. What will your children need to know to grow up and participate in the real world?

I have even suggested that a parent envision themselves moving west like the American pioneers in the 1800s. There are no schools, and no teachers. There may not even be a town where you are going. You will be raising children with only your own knowledge and a small stack of books.

What are the essentials?

They will need to know mathematic operations for home management and financial management. The ability to read, write, and spell is essential to all humans.

These are truly *the basics*. You can see why the "3 Rs" once made up the basic framework of an elementary education.

Now, a well-rounded person will also have a basic knowledge of the history of the world and the country of their birth. They will also understand and be familiar with basic scientific knowledge and thought, as well as arts and literature.

But the basics are where all of this begins.

In order to impart the basics to our children, a library card and internet access can truly suffice.

Even your small-town library will have a nice selection of history, science, art, and language books. Larger city libraries have so much more, such as videos, audiobooks, and even community classes and activities. Even if you don't have internet at home, access to library computers will open up the world wide web, which is the frugal homeschooler's best friend.

If expense is *not* an issue, of course parents have a wealth of wonderful, complete curriculum programs available. The rapid increase of homeschooling over the past thirty years has resulted in a wide array of curriculum options. There are literally hundreds of curriculum vendors that sell specifically to the homeschool parent. Boxed programs, complete with textbooks and teacher guides in each subject can be delivered to your door with the click of an online shopping cart.

But if you're reading this chapter in earnest, chances are you are looking for the budget-friendly options.

I have much experience in this area and after 20 years of homeschooling, I can promise you that a very basic set of materials is really all you need to educate children.

Let's examine the different levels of frugality:

Zero budget

Many parents feel that in order to begin homeschooling, they must find the perfect curriculum and have the school desks in place and a big whiteboard on the wall. While that would be a very comfortable way to start, it's not important.

As I stated before, working with very little money will mean that more of your time is necessary to find good materials. But if you believe your child would learn best in the home, it's absolutely worth your time.

Free resources abound on the web. Thanks to the world of bloggers, and the need for bloggers to grow their readership, there are tons of free educational resources available for download. Whether it's preschool counting or high school science, you can and will find lists of resources to create a complete curriculum.

There are entire websites devoted to compiling all the free homeschool curricula in one place! You can find links to them on my website.

Consider all the possibilities: YouTube videos, borrowed books from friends or the library, free curriculum from the web, free eBooks, documentaries, educational toys, online games and learning sites, and community events. With a basic plan, a parent can create a very rich learning experience with no curriculum expense.

The goal is to foster a love for learning and to encourage curiosity about the world around us. I have been in this boat, and no matter what we spent or did not spend, my children never stopped learning.

Let me encourage you that nothing lasts for long. You may be strapped for cash this year, but next year could look very different. Put your curriculum dreams on hold temporarily, but don't give in to despair.

A small budget

Let's say you do have a little money in the budget, and you'd like to purchase curriculum. There are some great companies that offer inexpensive books and resources, and the availability of used curriculum is wide.

Spend your money on the most important, or most difficult subject. Do you have a child ready to begin Algebra? You may want to find a good math curriculum for them, and supplement other subjects with free and online resources. But maybe YOU are proficient in math and feel confident to teach from any materials, and you'd rather focus on writing or science. Put your money toward those resources instead.

If possible, purchase non-consumable books (like the textbooks you're familiar with from your own school days). If you have more than one child, these can be used again with a stack of notebook paper or a cheap, spiral notebook.

Do you know other homeschoolers in your area? Ask if they will let you look at the books they are using. Do some window shopping. Many larger cities now have homeschool stores (these are not the same as "teacher" stores) that carry a nice selection of new and used curriculum. This allows you to make informed purchases instead of spending money on materials that you don't know much about.

For the best chance at seeing all the possible options, look for a homeschool convention in your region. These are held in large convention centers, and typically have an enormous vendor hall as well as speakers and workshops. You can see what every company offers, pick up the books and look through them, and even chat with the staff of the company. I think you'll be amazed.

A real budget

Maybe you're willing to spend whatever is necessary to educate your children. That's great! Spend wisely and be flexible. The biggest, most expensive program out there may not be the best one for your kids, or your family. Even with a comfortable spending amount, it's wise to make an informed decision on which curriculum best fits your students.

Again, I highly recommend a homeschool convention in your area. Become familiar with the different styles of home education and take a look at the different options.

If you are new to the homeschooling world, you may be absolutely shocked at the amount of materials available to you. It's our best-kept secret! These are not the same books used in public schools (with a very few exceptions). The companies have taken great advantage of the freedom of parents to educate their children and have provided so many options based on learning styles, budgets, special needs, religious focus, and more.

Free Online Curriculum

Complete, online, free homeschooling programs have skyrocketed in popularity recently. In fact, they are where many new homeschoolers first turn to begin their schooling. Free and online sounds like an incredible option, but there can be some drawbacks.

Sitting in front of a computer for several hours each day could take its toll on a child, especially if it does not suit their personality or learning style. It may make parents feel like much is being accomplished, by marking off lists and seeing their children complete units. But they also remove the parent involvement (which in my opinion, is very important). Additionally, they limit a child's exposure to "real" resources, like books, hands-on activities, and in some cases, actual writing.

Depending solely on this type of curriculum will often result in unintended behaviors, loss of interest, and burnout for both you and your child.

However, if you are on a strict budget or have other constraints (such as being a single parent or a working mom), free online schools might be the easiest option. If possible, consider an online option for one or two subjects, perhaps the most difficult ones.

Public School at Home

These programs are offered by various states and are typically free. They often include a computer, textbooks, and various supplies needed to complete each lesson. The family is required to follow the rules that come with this program, including logging in during "class hours," completing assignments on a certain schedule, taking state assessments, and reporting in regularly.

Carefully consider what *public school at home* means: bringing the same system home that *you chose to leave*. I personally do not recommend these programs for any reason, unless you live in a state that absolutely requires this and allows nothing else.

Here's why. You are choosing to leave the public school system for whatever reason. Don't leave it and then recreate it at home. These programs are usually free but come with the same strings attached as any government program. You are not in control of your time, your child's education, or your materials. The state is still in control. You may think I'm being overly harsh. Before you doubt me, do your research. Ask other parents who use these or have used them.

There are some great free alternatives to the public-school-at-home option, and they do not come with the state strings attached.

Having said all this, the great thing about home education is that the choices are many and the final decision is completely up to you. I present this information for you to consider. There is no wrong choice. Weigh the options and find what works best for your budget.

Visit *AnyoneCanHomeschool.net* for links to the resources mentioned here.

CHAPTER 4: SPECIAL NEEDS

Change your thinking: Regard the label 'learning disability' as signifying 'This child needs a different approach,' rather than 'Something is wrong with your child.'

-Susan Wise Bauer, Rethinking School

Having a child with special needs might just be the most intimidating part of homeschooling a child. We have been led to believe that only experts can solve the problems of children who are different than the "norm."

What *is* normal, anyway? Who gets to decide?

According to the public school system, normal means happily sitting in a desk all day while teachers tell you what you need to know. Normal means not getting fidgety, writing neatly (using the handwriting style decided by your state education agency), using curriculum that was also chosen by your state agency. Normal means playing for 15 minutes, twice a day. Normal means learning times tables by 3rd grade, and state history by 5th. Normal means checking off a list of accomplishments by age 18 and meeting the arbitrary standards set by your state (and sometimes federal) agency.

Normal means having "experts" tell you what your kids need, instead of being able to discern for yourself.

If your child does not fit into this "normal," they are given labels with all combinations of the alphabet. They are termed "special" and moved to different classrooms away from their "normal" peers. They are stigmatized. They are recommended for special therapies and drugs.

But what if your child, in your home, was free from the standards set by your state or federal agency? What if they were allowed to delay math instruction for a couple of years? What if they were allowed to recite times tables while jumping on the trampoline? What if they were allowed to function in their own "normal" and learn on a schedule that suits their physical and emotional abilities? What if they were allowed to do their spelling test verbally? What if they could put aside the workbooks for the day and listen to you read a great story while they created something with clay, or drew pictures, or built a tower of blocks, or worked with Legos? What if they could center their learning around a passion, such as airplanes, with a unit study?

The special needs child (no matter what that special need is) doesn't just *survive* comfortably in the homeschool environment; they can *thrive and excel*.

A Safe Place

Whether they have a physical disability, a learning challenge, or emotional issues, the home is their safe place. They can be who they are with the love and care of a parent while still getting an education. The family already knows how to accommodate the special-needs child. There is no need to have further special meetings, special classrooms, and constant interruptions to the school's flow because of flare-ups of any kind. In the home, that child has the freedom to have a great day or a bad day without "falling behind." In the home, the parent has the freedom to complete a full school day or to call it quits when the child is exhibiting signs of stress, without worrying about the school's calendar or requirements.

Before I proceed, I'll be totally honest. This is the one area of this book where I do not have personal experience.

I *do* have two boys, and based on my experience teaching them for the last 14 years, I feel certain they would be called ADD or ADHD simply because they bounce in their seat, stare out the window during math, or zone out when I am reading to them. I quickly determined that in order to keep their attention, I had to work with them in short spurts, broken up with physical activity; I had to teach them to take control of their thoughts by focusing on what they are doing.

In *Rethinking School*, Susan Wise Bauer notes:

According to the Centers for Disease Control and Prevention, boys are diagnosed with ADHD at three times the rate that girls are...I think that a lot of learning disability specialists don't realize how much preteen boys need to move around.[9]

My friend Lisa (read her story in Chapter 10) has a son who has dyslexia. She never felt that she couldn't homeschool. She says she just ignored the doubt and found a way. Her son is a visual learner, so they searched until they found a curriculum that worked for him. Her best advice: "Do your research and find what works best for your child." Oh, and, "Have patience!"

Now, I know that there are other, more concrete issues that parents and their children face. To address these fully, I have turned to many mothers I know who have found ways to surmount these obstacles and teach their children in a loving, safe environment at home.

Here is what works for them.

Tiffany

My friend Tiffany impressed me early on with her honesty in explaining her son's situation and her willingness to openly ask for help. So, I was excited when she agreed to share her story.

Her son is 10 years old and falls on the high-functioning side of the Autism Spectrum. He has a mood disorder call Disruptive Mood Dysregulation

Disorder, ADHD w/ impulsivity, dyslexia and dysgraphia. (She also has a seven-year-old daughter.)

Here's our interview:

Do you homeschool because of this particular child's needs or for more general reasons?

"We knew we would homeschool before our children were born. We wavered slightly through the toddler years on whether we would homeschool. As kindergarten approached, I realized there was no way that my special-needs child would succeed in a public school environment. We used a lot of non-traditional (if you consider public school education the tradition) education tools to teach things like counting and phonemic awareness. My son loved airplanes. His dad is a pilot, his grandparents were flight attendants, and his great grandfathers flew in World War 2. So, we went to the airport and counted airplanes. We looked for letters and numbers and colors on the planes. We used whatever subject he was most interested in and taught him all about it. We were able to give him a specialized kindergarten education that public school would not have been able to give him."

Tell me about a typical homeschool day. Do you have a strict schedule or go with the flow? Does your son use a typical curriculum, or do you use an eclectic mix? Does he sit at a desk or table, or find a more comfortable place to study?

"We start our day with the basics. We had a period of 3 years when our only hope was that our special needs child would reach adulthood and hopefully live on his own. We knew that might just mean a guest house on our property. So, we tried to teach him important life skills first. Wake up at a reasonable time (about 7:30 am). Brush your teeth, wash your face, eat breakfast, and get dressed, without having to be told to do those things. These are basic life skills that adults must do every morning without being told to do them.

After he takes care of the morning basics, he plays outside or builds with Legos or bounces on a yoga ball (anything that gets him moving and his brain working before school.) During this time, I work with his sister on her basics and then her math and reading. Our main focus during school is reading, writing, and math. We live on a farm and learn a lot of science through real life. History comes naturally as well. My husband has instilled a love for history by telling stories of battles his grandfathers fought in and by watching documentaries.

When my son is ready to start school (usually about 10 a.m.), he chooses which subject he wants to begin. He loves math, so that is usually where he starts. We have tried a lot of different math curriculums. Some have lots of color and pictures, some are teacher centered, some student centered. We landed on one made by the Amish. It has a lot of book work, and he is not able to write well. With Dyslexia and Dysgraphia, reading and writing have been a struggle. So, we compromised. I do not correct which direction his numbers go during math (that is an issue addressed in handwriting). There are 100 math problems per day. I ask him to do 10 addition/subtraction/multiplication/division problems. If he gets them all correct, he does not have to do any more. If he gets one wrong, then he does one more with my help so that I can correct whatever the issue is. If there are other kinds of math problems such as word problems, counting money, telling time, etc., then he only needs to do half of those problems.

We went slow with reading. We used Teach Your Child to Read in 100 Easy Lessons. Then we read books together. He would read the words he knew (a, I, and, the) and I would read the rest. One day, he suddenly recognized more words. At 9 years old, he suddenly began to read on his own. I remember the day he read a whole page without any help. He was suddenly a reader. So, we stopped using a reading curriculum and just let him read. He reads all kinds of books from Magic Tree House to history books, to novels and books of the Bible. He loves reading. I feel like this is my biggest accomplishment as a teacher. If he can read, he can learn anything.

While I am working with him on his math, reading, and writing, I also help my daughter with handwriting and let her do art or go play while I finish working with him. We work where he is able. Usually that is at the kitchen table. We have also done school under his bed (a hammock bed in his room), under a tree outside, and on the living room floor. We are usually done with school by lunch. My children make their own lunch. I feel that this is another basic skill they should have. They usually make a sandwich of some kind. If we are home for lunch, they may also choose to eat leftovers.

I have a part-time job. So, after school, which is usually after lunch or just before lunch, we go to work. I am an accountant and also manage the office of a construction and trailer-repair company. The company is very family oriented. They know that my child has special needs and some days I must work from home. I can go into work about three days a week.

My kids have learned about business management, customer service, and how to deal with employee issues. We have a company that comes and maintains a snack and soda machine. My children were there when they installed the machine and the owner let them program the machine. How many 2nd and 4th graders get to program a soda machine? I love that they learn real-life business skills. The company has a large show room where my children can ride bikes and play. They aren't required to sit quietly. They get to be children and learn naturally.

We usually work until 5:00 p.m. We then go home and get ready for end-of-day basics. The kids can help cook dinner (they love to help with dinner, but aren't required to), or they can play outside or in their rooms. After dinner, they clean their rooms, shower and brush teeth, and put themselves to bed. We go in and say goodnight but want them to know how to do a basic bedtime routine for themselves. As an adult, they will need to put themselves to bed at a reasonable hour. For us, right now, that hour is 8 p.m. So, we make sure they know their routine and it gets them in bed at about that time. My son reads in bed and recently has taken up drawing (which is huge since he has dysgraphia) until he is tired enough to fall asleep. He is usually asleep by 9:00 p.m."

When it comes to your son's specific needs, what have you found helpful for him? Are there any "out of the box" ideas you can share?

"There are some days when his mood is not conducive for learning. His brain is not fully functioning. His mood disorder literally causes the brain to begin shutting down and only the amygdala is fully functioning. That means that his brain is in "fight-or-flight" mode. His first instinct is flight. So, he is a runner. When you have a ten-year-old, almost as big as you are, fight-or-flight isn't something that you want to have to wrestle with. So, if he is on edge, we do not do school.

We school all year around so that we can take breaks when we need them. For him, this usually isn't a fall break or spring break, but a day here and there. For my daughter, she also takes a break when she needs it. These breaks do not always happen on the same day. There are some days when they are both fine, and I need a break. Homeschooling all year long allows us to take breaks when we need them."

What do you do when his specific challenge takes over and interrupts the school day?

"We stop. With him or with both children. If we are out somewhere, we have learned that we can stop there too. For example, if he is overwhelmed at a museum, I have a few choices:

1) *Leave. Even if we paid a huge fee for entry and we only stayed 30 minutes. It is better for my son's mental health to just leave. Leaving also causes less of a scene and less chance of property damage.*
2) *Find a dark, quiet place to go. Staff at most places understand special circumstances and will help you find a quiet place to calm down.*
3) *Find and accept help. If we are in full-blown meltdown, I may need help with my daughter while I deal with my son. This was a scary concept for me. There is usually another mom with kids in tow or a staff member that will ask if I need help. I used to say no. Every time. Now I say, "Yes. I just need you to chat with my daughter and distract her so that I can focus on my son."*

Sometimes, special needs are very hard on the siblings. You have to find a way to meet their needs, too. I believe that my daughter will be a very personable and compassionate person because she also knows how to diffuse a meltdown and explain to others what her brother deals with. It is okay to stop. And it is okay to ask for and accept help."

What kind of support system do you have?

"Support is very hard to find. It has only been the last two years that I really feel like I have a good team in place. My husband is the best part of my support system. It didn't happen overnight. It took marriage counseling, relationship classes, and even anger management for us to get to a place where we could handle the normal stresses of marriage compounded with the stress of having a special needs child.

I also have two friends who will babysit my kids. No other family will babysit because of my son's disorder. One friend is a homeschooler with a special-needs child of her own. She gets it. She knows what we are going through and is willing to take on my kids from time to time. The other is a mom of three who loves and accepts us as we are.

I am also blessed by a large homeschool community that accepts us. We have stopped homeschool enrichment classes for now, but when we were in them, our homeschool group went above and beyond to accommodate our needs. I was able to attend his classes. Those classes had extra helpers. The hallway monitors knew to watch for and hopefully catch my son if he ran. There were times when his meltdown happened very loudly in the hallway. The other families understood our situation and would keep their class focused so that I didn't have to worry about people staring at us or other people getting hurt.

My church has also been a huge help. We do not have a special-needs program, but they have set up a room for us to watch the service on a monitor. We can hear, watch, and worship freely. We have a pediatric occupational therapist that goes to our church. She volunteers to work with my son as his special helper for events like VBS. She is also available as needed. She is such a huge blessing to our family. It allows me to serve and allows for my children to learn about God and His love from someone other than my husband and me."

What kind of encouragement can you give to other parents who want to homeschool but feel that it would be too hard with a special-needs child?

"You are the best teacher for your child. No teacher will love him or care about his education as much as you do. Homeschooling does not mean that your child will be at a public school education level or higher. It means teaching your child at your child's level. That may mean that your child only learns basic skills, and that is okay."

Do you notice how Tiffany has structured a life that works for her son? School schedule, outings, bedtime...all of it is set up to help him thrive. In your own home, you can do this. Your home doesn't have to look like your neighbor's home, just like your school doesn't have to look like all the other schools.

Bauer has a great chapter in her book *Rethinking School* called "Differences, Disabilities, and Disorders." She talks about getting these diagnosed, what they look like, and how they are addressed:

...notice that in almost every case, the therapy involved is essentially: Teach in a different way, teach skills explicitly, target the area where the student needs more work and support. Technically that's not treatment. It's just good teaching.

Good teaching is responsive to the student, flexible, always experimenting, equipped with a full toolbox of strategies that make sense to different kinds of brains, and creative enough to find multiple ways to present information and train skills.

Yet no matter how gifted the teacher, it is practically impossible to offer this kind of teaching to a large, understaffed classroom of widely differing learners, particularly in a school where the curriculum is inflexible, test-centered, and/or tied to strictly defined outcomes at specific grade levels." [10]

This is why, in most cases, home education is actually a better way to raise a child with special needs.

Now, meet another friend, Jayne, with a special needs son.

Jayne

How many children do you homeschool with special needs? What are their ages?

"One with special needs, and another who is on the spectrum, but fits into the general school population now."

What is the nature of the special need?

"It's undiagnosed (since the brain is complicated, they cannot diagnose every kid with a Pervasive Development Disorder, PDD); but he's got dyslexia, sensory, auditory, and short/mid-term memory issues, speech delays, and delays in other areas."

Do you homeschool because of this particular child's needs, or for more general reasons?

"More general. When we realized he had special needs, we were all the more determined, as it was definitely a better fit."

Tell me about a typical homeschool day. Do you have a strict schedule or go with the flow? Does your child use a typical curriculum, or do you use an eclectic mix? Does your child sit at a desk or table or find a more comfortable place to study?

"In some ways, he needs a strict structure for meals, school-time, activities, and bedtime. But for school, we go with the flow curricula-wise. I had a plan with the 3 R's as a basis, and we'd go from there. We follow our books, but I have to be flexible on when to deviate to spend more time on something to help it stick, or to come up with some way to explain so he can "see" what I am saying. Everything took/takes more iterations...but some things really stick once he gets them."

When it comes to your child's specific needs, what have you found helpful for them? Are there any "out of the box" ideas you can share?

"Patience, flexibility, teaching to their needs, but being firm on what you will not bend on. This goes for food, sleep... being gentle without sounding angry or impatient (this was really a challenge when he was little and would try every last nerve!). Some things we had to go over again and again and again (like borrowing and carrying), even after he got them. Poetry helped with his speech and with reading (he has a great memory with things like this); it was an enormous help, and we didn't do watered-down poems. A Child's Garden of Verses is a staple. The author really gets kids and captures my boy's attention.

Limit video games and media. I can't emphasize this enough. It's hard enough to hold his attention and it could have ruined his desire to read and to imagine. The poetry idea for me would not have been a breakthrough if we had done a lot of media.

Cursive: my boy has dyslexia, and for a while, he could read that better than print. He struggled with fine motor skills and the practice (loops and curls, etc.) were great to get him used to writing without it being too precise. It's a brain thing, too.

Don't worry about other kids. My boy was a late reader, and if he was in school or with another teacher, they might have just chalked him up as not being a reader. Well, he's 14 and is an avid reader. I never, ever, ever thought I'd give him Goosebumps books, but that is what it took. And I only gave it to him when I thought he was mature enough and had a strong enough foundation for his faith. So, he can see the bad behaviors of kids in the books -- something he might have emulated when he was younger. He has a strong sense of good and evil and right and wrong. That is huge, in my opinion. Kids like my boy are easily very into media, so we were very, VERY careful about violent games or TV shows. I read stories of violent kids with autism and I wonder about their parents' choices in reading and media."

What do you do when their specific challenge takes over and interrupts the school day?

"We take breaks. Sometimes, they are just full and can't do more --and they can act out at you, the teacher. It's hard not to take it personally, but both of you need to maintain an open relationship, so your child knows they can count on you. I strongly recommend Attachment Parenting."

What kind of support system do you have?

"I didn't have any for so many years. I do now, but it's homeschooling in general. It would have been nice to have other parents with these kinds of issues. Now I do, but they are younger, so I can't really go to them for advice. Plus, PDDs are so different in nature with all of the different manifestations. Over the years, I'd run across a parent here and there whose child would have similar quirks. Mine loves Halloween and scary things. Again, we've always been careful, but have had to find a new balance.

This is something other mothers have with their PDD boys. It was affirming if nothing else."

What kind of encouragement can you give to other parents who want to homeschool but feel that it would be too hard with a special needs child?

"YOU know your child best. We moms have an instinct that isn't made-up -- it's a real, God-given gift. I shudder to think what would have happened had my boy been left in the care of "experts". No expert will love a child's heart and soul like mom (if the mom really has the best intentions, right?). It hurts my heart when I see parents with special-needs children and they are in denial. Our kids know they are different. If we accept it, we can talk about it, so our peers and their peers know, and it's freeing really. But it should not be used as a crutch for bad behavior. I'm seeing some special needs kids with no boundaries, now. That is not okay, either.

I cannot stress this enough: parents know their children better than the most gifted and most dedicated teacher. Parents spend time with their children in all situations and have learned through trial and error what works for them. The child's education is no different.

You can do this.

There is a wonderful community of homeschooling families with special needs of all kinds. There are moms and dads who have gone before you and have figured out the different needs, the curriculum, the tricks, the schedules, and so much more.

One more book I recommend for parents of children with any special needs is *Different* by Sally and Nathan Clarkson. It was written by a mother-son team about Nathan's special needs and how his parents learned to love and parent him through those needs.

AnyoneCanHomeschool.net has a list of helpful resources for navigating the special needs homeschool.

Chapter 5: The Single Parent

For so long I prayed that our family would be reconciled and once again fit into that perfect homeschooling family mold. But God has gently taught me that the perfect homeschooling family doesn't exist. He's taught me that I can still homeschool in the broken world because we are all broken, even those who aren't showing it.

-Kim Sorgius, NotConsumed.com

    Besides having a small budget, this seems to be the biggest brick wall that many parents *think* they face in homeschooling. It is another area in which I have personal experience, and I also know many single parents who successfully homeschool.

    I won't lie. It's not a breeze. In fact, I remember my single parent years as the hardest years of my life. I did not feel like an empowered woman. Not even close! I was doing the job of two parents and it was not easy.

So, when I say that a single parent can homeschool their children, I don't say it lightly. It takes a lot of determination and the strong conviction that this is what's best for your family. I want to tell you that it can be done, and that it is absolutely worth it!

My Story

I began my single mom journey without a dime to my name. I had my car, two little girls, and the belongings we took from our home. I literally had to start over.

I was fortunate to have a place to stay, as my mom and dad were building a home for retirement. It was still under construction, but it was livable. My daughters and I relocated to Oklahoma to take advantage of that home, and I began looking for work.

Oh, the struggle. We had one year of homeschooling behind us, and I was determined not to give that up. So, I needed a job that would allow us to continue.

At first, I did an odd assortment of small jobs, such as cleaning a church and childcare. In this way my daughters could go with me to work. After a couple of months of this, I found a part-time position as a medical transcriptionist at a local hospital and hired a wonderful lady to come care for my girls each afternoon while I worked. She treated them like grandchildren and did educational activities with them. I dabbled in other opportunities, such as teaching scrapbooking classes at a local craft store and transcribing from home.

And then one day I saw a "for sale" sign in a craft mall near me. I inquired, explored the possibilities of being my own boss, fell in love with the idea, and took the plunge. I made this decision based on one thing: my desire to raise my children myself. With this business, they could be with me at the store, do their schoolwork, and not spend their days with a babysitter.

It did work. Oh, the business didn't last forever, thanks to the economy and other factors. But we continued life as a family unit. We lived life together, working, schooling, eating, and having fun. We had a room at the back of the store just for their things, which included toys, a TV and DVD player, and even a twin bed for naps. Our store had a very relaxed environment (after all, it was a craft store) so my daughters spent lots of time in the storefront with me, sometimes doing schoolwork and sometimes just playing.

Though the business did not work out after a couple of years, I do not have a single regret about the decision. I was determined that home education was best for my girls, that it was a natural extension of my parenting. I did not have to give that up.

My girls are all grown up now, but we have some fun memories of even those tough times, and some very sweet memories, too. I do not regret spending as much time with them as possible, despite our difficult circumstances.

Since those years, I have a very soft place in my heart for the single parent who wants to homeschool. Having this experience myself, I always encourage them that, with conviction and flexibility, it can be done. It's one of the reasons I wrote this book.

I have a friend who is raising four daughters alone, and she has learned to be bold when it comes to sharing her needs. I asked her for some specifics on how she makes it work...

Dianna

My friend Dianna is a single mom to 4 daughters. She was homeschooling them for several years before she became a single mom. So, I asked her, "What made you choose to continue homeschooling as a single mom?"

Dianna told me, "I could visualize what they would experience in public school. It was already hard when they first attended, for various individual reasons. It would be even harder during a divorce."

She also pointed out that, though she and her daughters are busy and fairly exhausted a lot of the time, public school schedules combined with after-school activities would keep them just as busy, but family time would be almost non-existent. With Dianna's flexible job schedule, she has more time with her daughters. Having experienced both public school and homeschool lifestyles, she feels that she would just be trading one kind of stress for another.

And because divorce is not easy for anyone, she is very thankful for the ability that she has to be available to her daughters when they need to talk, cry, or vent their feelings. A child doesn't have to experience their roller coaster of emotions in a classroom with bottled-up feelings; it can happen at home with caring family members and a break from the bookwork.

So how does she accomplish everything?

At first, Dianna worked a couple of different part-time jobs that gave her schedule flexibility. She worked as a self-contracted cleaner for homes and businesses, so she had the option to bring her daughters along with her sometimes. Her days off work varied, so each day of the week looked different. She added Uber driving to her resume. It allowed her to utilize down time to earn money on a moment's notice.

Recently, Dianna accepted an office position with a flexible and understanding boss. She brings her children to work with her, where they do schoolwork, read, play with the children of another (homeschool mom) co-worker, and play on their tablets. She can leave to take a child to a class, or work from home when the need arises. It's been a huge blessing to her and the girls!

Dianna depends on the generosity of friends at church and in the homeschool community who provide occasional childcare, rides to activities, and playdates for her daughters.

She suggests that planning is key. Planning ahead with written assignments (especially for the older girls) keeps everyone focused on a goal. They are involved with 2 homeschool co-ops, but Dianna has made sure that her personal responsibility is very small. At one co-op she can just be there as a helper. Eeven lunch is provided in the co-op fees. And in the other co-op she is the cleaning coordinator, so there is no prep involved during the week.

Also, Dianna heavily utilizes 21st century technology. She has everything scheduled on her phone's calendar and even blocks out part of her schedule each day for school time to avoid getting overbooked. For the kids, electronic devices are a lifesaver (though she has a love-hate relationship with them, like a lot of parents!). The girls use some educational apps, and of course they enjoy some entertainment on their tablets, too. This dedicated mother says that her circumstances just require some things that she wouldn't like in a perfect world, but the overall family togetherness is worth certain sacrifices.

Dianna's oldest daughter took advantage of the dual-credit program at her local junior college. She was able to earn both high school and college credit for a very low cost, and participate in the college band, as well, with little planning or personal responsibility on Dianna's part.

There are definitely days when Dianna faces doubts. She says it would be so easy to put them back in school. Sometimes she thinks she's failing as a mom and a teacher. But she has learned to lower her expectations of what a perfect homeschool should look like. She says, "We are not one of those families that can volunteer for community projects right now. We don't do all the crafty stuff. We're in survival mode. Accepting that is *key*."

She has learned to tell herself that school happens when and where it's possible, no matter what time of day or year it is. She also reminds herself that this is just a season, and seasons can change.

By the way, Dianna's oldest daughter has graduated from homeschooling and is pursuing a college degree!

So how can *you* make home education work as a single parent?

Determine Your WHY

At the beginning, I advise all parents to start with a goal. Write down your WHY. Why do you want to homeschool? What is the need? (More on this in Part 2.)

This is especially important for the single parent. This *WHY* is going to be your inspiration during the tough times. Because being a single parent is already tough, and it gets a little tougher when you add in the responsibility for the education of your children.

Next, let's explore the common issues that single homeschooling parents face.

Finances

Being a single parent means providing financially, all alone, while still having time for every other aspect of parenting. Somehow you must earn money to survive. Now that you want to homeschool, you must determine how to continue earning money, how and when to put on your teacher hat, and figure out how to pay for educational materials.

We've already addressed homeschooling on a budget in Chapter 1, so let's talk about work.

You most likely already have a source of income, and now you're wondering how to manage home education on top of it. There are several options, and I hope at least one of these will fit your needs. It may require finding a new or different job that will accommodate your choices.

- Work from home. In this age of virtual commutes, more and more companies are open to their employees working at home. Depending on your position and the company you work for, an honest heart-to-heart conversation with your employer might result in a change of location, while you perform the same duties. You won't know unless you ask! Search online job postings

or look for companies that hire work-from-home employees. There are many positions for customer service reps who work from home, as well as online teachers.
- Change work hours. Sometimes a different shift at work makes all the difference at home. Working the night shift (with a night sitter at home) might allow you to sleep early in the morning and then have school. Consider what your company has available and what could make childcare or schooling easier. Will grandparents be willing to watch your children? Maybe working around their schedule is the answer.
- Be your own boss. This is a broad statement, but it's what so many single homeschooling parents turn to. Whether it's a house-cleaning business, a daycare in your home, or a skill you are trained in, consider self-employment. Maybe you can have a home-based business, an online venture, or a brick and mortar storefront.
- Bring your kids to work. Yes, this is possible! I've done it, and I have friends who do the same. Some work environments are naturally accommodating to children. If your children are old enough to work in schoolbooks on their own, this is very doable.

Most of these suggestions will only be available in specific types of industries or companies and will require some thinking out of the box. They may require special requests of your boss. Start brainstorming and don't give up!

Find a supportive community

Before we get to the practical stuff, let me tell you how important it is to connect with a homeschool support group in your area. Getting to know other families is important when homeschooling, but it is vital to a single parent.

I was already part of a homeschool community when my life as a single mom began. And there were other single moms who had already traveled this road. They inspired me. I knew that it was possible because I had seen them do it.

Developing friendships builds a network that is helpful when you have questions, need ride shares, need to buy or sell used curriculum, and need to find out about income opportunities. You will find out about learning cooperatives near you, possible childcare, and even random classes that your kids might attend.

While online support groups are helpful and informative, they can only go so far. Knowing people personally is where the real support happens. Talk to people at your church, at the library, wherever you go; find local homeschoolers and get connected. They are everywhere!

Curriculum

The next obvious question is, "How will I teach under my circumstances?" Thankfully, you live in a booming age for curriculum options. Flexibility is key here. You may find yourself choosing an option that might not be your first pick in an ideal world. But with an open mind, the possibilities are endless.

Traditional homeschooling is what you might envision: mom or dad sitting with the child and their books, reading aloud, helping with math work, and quizzing spelling words. If you have a work-at-home position, this is very doable.

But as you know, traditional circumstances are not often found in the home of a single parent. So, what other options are there? You actually have quite a few, depending on your budget, your schedule, and the ages of your children.

Online classes can fulfill your need for one subject or the entire curriculum. The choices run the full spectrum from free kindergarten curriculum to purchased high school curriculum. You can even find educational YouTube channels with very high-quality content for many subjects.

Virtual schools are those that provide all the instruction and additionally provide grading, testing, and transcript services. This takes most of the responsibility off the parent, while still allowing school to take place wherever necessary. If your child moves back and forth between two locations, school can continue fairly seamlessly.

DVD and CD curriculum presents video lectures, demonstrations, and assignments on computers and television. In homeschool math, there are two great examples of this style of curriculum: Math U See and Teaching Textbooks. They are both very different in their presentation and approach, but they both offer a valuable service to parents: complete math instruction. This is just one example among many.

University model schools and learning co-ops allow the parent to continue to oversee a child's education while providing classroom experiences with other children. The types of classes in this category vary widely and will depend on where you live.

Generally, a co-op is a cooperative organization that requires a parent to be on the premises as a volunteer. But there are many that do not have this rule and often make it easy for the child of single parents to participate. You'll find everything from core subjects to extra-curriculars in these groups.

A university model school is a sort of part-time private school where students attend classes 2 or 3 days per week and complete assignments at home on the other days. If you are a teacher, you might find that this could be a double bonus, in that you can get a job teaching in this type of program, while allowing your children to attend.

Tutors are a great option for subjects where a child needs extra help or when you know someone who is very knowledgeable in a certain subject. A high schooler, a college student, or an adult in your area can provide valuable help in a difficult subject.

Child Care

Normally, only working parents of pre-school aged children consider childcare options. But if you are a single parent and work outside the home, it gets a bit tricky. Where will your children be while you work?

We've touched on a couple of ideas under the headings of money and curriculum. If you have a job situation that accommodates you and your children, childcare may not be an issue right now.

But what if you work outside the home? Again, it's time to think outside the box.

If you have teenagers, you have babysitters. And it may be time for them to take on a bit more responsibility. If they are old enough to babysit for your neighbors, they are old enough to stay home alone (or to care for younger siblings). This does not mean they must teach school, but in certain situations, older siblings do enjoy helping younger ones with their learning.

Are grandparents nearby? Would they be willing to help? Perhaps they could come to your house and possibly even help with some schooling. I know families for whom this works beautifully. If you work the night shift, maybe the children can spend the night with grandparents or other relatives.

Without the option of teenagers or grandparents, paid babysitting might be necessary. It was for me during a certain period of single motherhood. If you search, you may be able to hire someone from your local homeschool group, whether it's another mom or a teenager. This is a great option because they understand the home education choice and will be sympathetic to your needs.

Time Management

As you are most certainly aware, this is tricky for a single parent. Juggling a household, a job, and parenting make for a pretty full plate. Adding education to this mix will mean penciling in even more in your day.

To be honest, I never made it all work perfectly. I had to take one day at a time, and you will, too. Sometimes I felt overwhelmed and exhausted. Sometimes I thought I couldn't do it. I prayed all day, every day. You probably will, too. But there are also a few practical ways to reduce the stress you're under.

Pray: God is your strength and a very present help in trouble (Psalm 46:1). In my time as a single mom, my prayer life was one of desperation. I "cried out" to the Lord most of the time. And He was there to strengthen me through the hard, faith-building times.

All these years later, I look back and realize just how much my faith in God grew during those difficult times. I kept a journal of my prayers, my needs, and God's answers, and it is still a blessing to this day to see how faithfully God provided!

Slow-cooking: My favorite time-saver and stress-saver is slow cooking. I use my slow-cooker even now, but it's a lifesaver for a busy parent. With a good stack of easy recipes and a slow-cooker, you can provide hot meals that don't cost an arm and a leg, and you can avoid fast food more often. You can do everything from bean soup to smoking a brisket in your slow cooker. It's such a great feeling to know that dinner is cooking itself. Oh, and don't forget breakfast. I love to use my slow cooker overnight to make a big, hot breakfast! Go to the internet for inspiration: friends, social media groups, and recipe websites all have tons of delicious ideas.

Meal planning: Planning anything at all is going to make your life easier, but planning meals for a week or two in advance reduces mental stress (the stress can be huge!), saves money, and saves time. If your kids are old enough, let them help you. Jot down your favorite meals and be sure to include plenty of quick and easy-to-prepare options. From this menu plan, create your grocery shopping list.

Additionally, make full use of modern conveniences like paper plates and grocery pickup or delivery. Set up your grocery list on the grocery store website and schedule a pickup after work. You'll save yourself hours of trudging through busy stores at the end of an exhausting work day. Plus, as you're writing out your weekly meal plan, you can add grocery items to your online cart all in the same planning session.

Chore training: Because you've got a complicated lifestyle, you need help. No matter what age your children are, training them to help with basic household chores is imperative. It's important for every family, but it's going to be a game changer for the single parent. Little toddlers love to help and it's a perfect age to begin training them. They want to feel important, and they will listen and learn. It's a wonderfully teachable age. Older kids may already have a couple of chores, but now it's time for them to move beyond making their beds and feeding the dog.

Schedule a free day to discuss the needs of the household and assign new jobs to each member of the family based on their age and ability. Spend the first few weeks training, watching, and checking their work. Before long, they will help you run a fairly smooth household and you will have more time to enjoy the fun things with them! Consider a reward for a job well done, such as a movie night in the living room with fresh baked brownies, or pizza for dinner on cleaning day.

FUN! Be sure you take time to have fun. This means that sometimes everything I've just mentioned will be put on hold (chores, cooking, etc.) and you and the kids enjoy yourselves for awhile. Surprise them with donuts early on a school morning. Get out to the park with a picnic and your history book. Make cookies in the middle of the day. Declare a "board game day". Have a theme day at home or something fun to look forward to each week. (I once read about a mom who did "chocolate milk Fridays," which was a big deal since the kids didn't drink it the rest of the week.) You, as the single parent, need a break from the crazy schedule, and your kids need to see you having fun and joining in.

Getting it all done will look different for every single parent. Make a plan, set it in motion, and reassess it from time to time. As I said before, things change, and hard times get better. Kids grow up. Circumstances change. It won't always be difficult.

Think about the long term. Build relationships with your children. Create memories.

Ask for Help

It's okay to admit when you need help. We all need help sometimes. And I can think of no other person who needs more help than a homeschooling single parent. Whether you need help with childcare, carpooling, curriculum ideas, laundry, meal prep, or just need a friendly ear, it's imperative that you do not travel this journey in a vacuum.

Don't be afraid to ask for help. For some, this is much easier to do than for others. But be honest about your needs and desires. Connect with other homeschooling parents and share your desire for home education, and share what needs you have.

CHAPTER 6:
THE "UNQUALIFIED" PARENT

The National Home Education Research Institute reports that children who are educated at home typically score 15 to 30% higher than public school students on standardized academic achievement tests. This is true of students who are taught by parents with or without a formal education, and students whose parents fall within a wide range of income brackets. In other words, a parent's education and financial standing have no bearing on a homeschooled student's ability to score higher on standardized tests than children who attend a public school.[11]

We live in a world of "experts". They are everywhere, and we are convinced we need them for all aspects of our lives. And parenting experts are the scariest. The experts and their cheerleaders would have us believe that moms and dads aren't equipped to make any decisions on their own, and if they do, children will be victims of abuse and neglect.

So let's bust the myth right now that every parent must have a degree in multiple fields in order to raise healthy, well-adjusted children, or that they must pay someone else to walk them through every stage. This includes the area of education.

I'm a huge believer in parents being the experts on their own children. You know your kids better than anyone out there, including their doctor, the teachers, the coaches, and even their grandparents. As I mentioned in a previous chapter, you taught them everything they needed to know up until Kindergarten. Why stop now?

You are the most qualified teacher of your child

Claiming that *anyone* can homeschool is really no different than saying "Anyone Can Cook" or "Anyone Can Knit." Sure, there are well-educated experts who cook and knit, but there are also lots of self-taught cooks and knitters. They seek out information and get their hands dirty figuring it all out.

The reality is that parents do this every day. Think about the parent who has suspected an allergy or medical problem with their child. Despite multiple doctor or hospital visits, there are times when doctors can't find the cause, and a parent is left with more questions than answers. These parents do enough research to become experts in a new and unfamiliar field. Why? *Because parents will go to the ends of the earth to do what's best for their children.* A concerned parent will lose sleep, spend money, and give up everything to help their child out of a difficult situation.

Don't be alarmed: schooling your child is not nearly as hard as finding a rare medical diagnosis, but you get the idea. Parents are a capable and determined bunch, and with the tools available to us in the 21st century, there is no need to fear the education world.

Remember: certified teachers spend a lot of their college education learning classroom management and communication. Only a portion is spent on the specifics of teaching the core subjects.

What I want you to take from this is that *you are more than qualified to teach your child*, even with the barest education. You have a personal, intimate connection coupled with the natural parental desire to give your child the best of everything. The most devoted classroom teacher under the sun cannot begin to match your dedication.

If you can read, you can teach

My own mother taught me at home when homeschooling was new and considered very weird. When I had finished up the 5th grade at our local public school, she and my dad made the decision that my sister and I would be schooled at home from there on out.

And my mom didn't finish the 9th grade.

She didn't have a high school diploma, let alone a college degree. She also didn't have access to the internet or the tons of helps available to homeschool parents today. It was the 1980's! But she could read, and she was a concerned mom. So she just buckled down and did it.

How? How is it even possible for a parent without a complete education to teach their own children?

It's possible because if you can read, you can teach. If you can read, you can learn what you don't know.

And you know, I have a college degree and I still find myself looking up things that my children need to know.

Ask yourself: who really has all the knowledge in the world? Does the best teacher have all the answers? Does the most educated college professor know everything there is to know? No. Because everyone has a specialty, and though some teachers may excel in many areas, they cannot possibly excel in all. And that means they must search for answers, too.

If you're willing to find the information you don't already have, you can teach your children.

Let me just say, "Welcome to homeschooling!" In this world, you don't have to figure out the state-issued textbooks and teacher's guides. In this world, you choose the curriculum that works for your family, and trust me: it's easy. In fact, it's kind of addicting. You will soon see that browsing curriculum catalogs might be your new favorite hobby.

There are numerous wonderful curriculum companies who cater to a wide variety of learning styles and teaching styles. Remember: homeschoolers have flexibility. We have the freedom to try new things, to seek out resources that best fit our family.

You may have a little math whiz in your family, but math scares you to death. Or maybe you love math but you're afraid you won't know how to teach it to your child. There are excellent materials with video instruction or online demonstrations that walk both the student and parent through the math problems.

Maybe you are an English nerd, but your child can't spell to save his life, and you can't figure out why! There are companies that produce an amazing array of different language arts programs to cater to every learning style, or even learning struggles.

Don't be concerned if you don't remember Chinese history, European geography, or even the names of the continents.

You are not a professor; *you are the facilitator.*

Let me bring up freedom again. Freedom is what makes homeschooling so wonderful. You're not tied to the same curriculum the schools use. You're not tied to one curriculum for every subject. And you're not even tied to your house for each class.

It is amazing!

Homeschoolers have the freedom to seek out a tutor, a class, or a learning cooperative to fill in some of the gaps or to teach the hard subjects. A parent who is just not confident in algebra (like me!) has the freedom to find someone who is. An online class may provide just what a family needs for a literature study or science class.

It's like ordering from the *a la carte* menu. You pick the best resources, teachers, and groups from a variety of options to create your child's school schedule. Depending on where you live, the options are many.

I live in a very rural area of North Texas. But even with our seemingly impossible location, my children have had numerous opportunities to take classes outside our home. My oldest daughter has attended science classes in the home of a public-school-teacher-turned-homeschool-mom, and a writing class at a local library taught by another homeschool mom. My sons are taking weekly middle-and-high school science classes taught by friends of ours who are retired teachers and homeschool parents.

Prepare to Re-educate Yourself

There is a bonus to homeschooling that parents discover after they've had a year or two under their belt: re-education. Those subjects that they forgot, or hated, or maybe never learned are suddenly fun and interesting. I cannot even count the times I've heard a homeschool mom say, "I'm having so much fun learning again!"

Becoming a teacher doesn't mean that you stand at the whiteboard and give lectures and grade papers. If you are a homeschool parent, you can get involved in the learning in so many different ways: teach the material, read stories aloud, look up problems and solve them together, have conversations about interesting facts you've learned, and facilitate hands-on activities.

Some days we do encounter difficult questions in a lesson or problems we can't solve. Guess what? This is a normal part of life. It's a great time to teach your children how to search for answers, and how to put something away for another time. We've done both, numerous times. Go to the internet, or the library, or to a knowledgeable friend or family member.

Educating your children will increase your own education. You'll transform from feeling inadequate and hesitant to being an expert on many subjects. Ask me how I know!

Outside Sources

In my rural area in far north Texas the population of my entire county is just over 39,000. But there are some great opportunities available for homeschoolers here. Over the past 15 years, we've had writing intensive classes taught at our local library, high school math classes taught by a pastor, writing clubs, history field trips, geography co-ops led by moms, robotics teams through 4H, and science classes complete with labs for all ages. Our local homeschool cooperative has offered classes in everything imaginable, including cooking, Irish dance, algebra tutoring, color guard, ultimate frisbee, psychology, government and economics, coffee, horsemanship, personal finance, and so much more. There are currently three different homeschool cooperatives in a 15 mile distance from my rural home.

Besides joining other homeschoolers for classes outside the home, consider the possibility of what you can offer inside your own home.

Virtual online classes are gaining in popularity. With an internet connection, the world is literally your classroom. Many homeschool curriculum companies offer the additional service of live classes, taught by the teachers and creators of their company. Whether you choose one subject (because you're not comfortable teaching it) or the entire list of subjects, you'll have experts in every area available at the click of a mouse.

Math and science have always been the subjects that many seek extra help in. We've used Math-U-See for over a decade and love the video instruction (along with the optional online classes). Science video courses through The 101 Series as well as Supercharged Science have given me real peace of mind in this important subject.

Guest teachers and home groups are another easy (and fun) way to bring in help. As far back as the 1980's we did this in our family. My parents would invite members of our church to come for a weekly "chapel service" in our home, and my aunt and cousins would join us. When I reached the high school years, my uncle would tutor me in math and science. (Remember: my mom didn't finish her high school education, so she found ways to outsource some of the teaching even then.) Currently, that same uncle is joining our family for some history lessons, complete with local field trips, class lectures in my living room, and reading assignments in between. And we've even invited a few extra kids to join us for these special events.

Don't just take my word for it...

I interviewed some homeschool parents on how they found outside help for different aspects of education, and I'm happy to share some of their ideas:

- Numerous moms have utilized learning co-ops, which come in many forms.
- My kids have attended writing classes at our local library, science classes at the home of another homeschool family, and participated in drama at the community theater. My second daughter took French with a video course from Switched-On-Schoolhouse.
- Music teachers such as piano, voice teacher, and classical guitar teachers.
- A Texas mom used a Barton tutor to teach her dyslexic daughter reading. She had such high anxiety related to reading that it affected their learning environment at home.
- Many parents utilize a combination of resource classes, online classes, co-op, dual credit college classes, private tutoring, and private lessons.

- For some parents, farming out science is a must – especially as kids get older. Let the science teacher take care of dissections!
- Find online classes for foreign language so students experience a native speaker.
- Look for speech and debate with a local speech club.
- A friend from Florida says, "We have a private school that is only for homeschoolers. It runs like a university model. Show up for class and do everything else at home. You pay by the class and choose how many classes to take. It is fully accredited as a traditional school."
- One friend of mine takes her kids to English classes at Friday School: A tutor teaches the classes one day of the week with a week full of homework. They also utilized the Boy Scouts Eagle Scout program for many learning activities.
- There is a mobile science lab based in Texas, called HiScience. It is a 2-day lab intensive for chemistry and biology.
- A homeschool grad in my area utilized a video-based program for Algebra class. Other homeschool kids in our area attended Algebra classes taught by a local pastor.
- A childhood friend of mine discovered a private art teacher through a homeschool Facebook page.

- Another family I know takes classes online through the Potter's School and Homeschool Legal Defense Association, where you may choose one or more classes to fit your needs and pay only for the classes you choose.
- Even small communities offer opportunities such as STEM and PE classes.
- Numerous families in our area have joined the Oklahoma Homeschool Band where they learn instruments and hold performances a couple of times each year.
- A former teacher friend of mine recommends Classes by Beth Plus live online classes for Geometry, Biology, Writing, and Ethics.
- Anther homeschool grad I know joined a local gymnastics class (and it led to opening his own gym and running his own business!).
- When a local friend's daughter wanted to learn sign language, they paid a private tutor who lived two states away to teach American Sign Language through Skype.
- Multiple kids join martial art classes in their town.

And my friend Linda summed it up perfectly: *"All of the above. Homeschooling offers the opportunity to select the best resources for every subject to match the child's individual needs and learning style. It was great for them and engaged them with other students and teachers."*

You may have noticed something else that comes with these options: socialization! That's the double bonus. Homeschool families are all around you; you just have to seek them out!

Remember: you are not a school. You are *rethinking school*. You can see that with a little creativity and some searching, the options are endless. And they are fun. Don't give up before you've started.

There's one very important thing to add to all these great ideas: each one was begun by a parent who saw a need and decided to step up and meet it. Homeschool parents are resourceful. So, as a beginner, take advantage of the great opportunities in your area, but don't stop there. Help to start or coordinate something that's lacking: volunteer your kitchen for a class, offer to teach weekly music classes, help start a book club, call around and find a willing teacher for science labs, or help form a learning cooperative in your town. Don't wait around for someone else to do it! Get that ball rolling and others will join you!

CHAPTER 7:
CHRONIC ILLNESS IN THE FAMILY

We can get too easily bogged down in the academic part of homeschooling, a relatively minor part of the whole, which is to raise competent, caring, literate, happy people.

- Diane Flynn Keith

Sometimes parents suffer from chronic illness; sometimes their child does. In both situations, home education is very possible, and is often beneficial. As with many subjects in this book, I have personal experience.

My life with chronic migraines

Since the age of 8, headaches have been a normal part of my life. They began in childhood as "normal" headaches (if you can call them that!) and became full-blown migraines in my teen years. Mine are triggered by stress, heat, skipping meals, hormones, and certain types of pollen. This means they are largely unpredictable.

A typical migraine for me lasts a minimum of 24 hours but can last as long as 3 days. I am mostly incapacitated during this time but can also occasionally sit in the living room to supervise the activities of my children. I cannot read books or screens with a migraine because of the pain it causes my eyes. So, you can see how it affects our schooling.

Since I had migraines before I had children, I learned a few things about parenting with the pain. The most important thing I learned early on was to relax my standards. As far back as my first newborn I quickly realized that I could either be devastated by the effect migraines had on my motherhood, or I could adapt. I learned to adapt.

Adapting, for us, meant that my kids were going to need to learn some independence. Independence is the key to keeping our house under control while mom is ill. You might guess that this doesn't just apply to schooling. But if you've read the first two chapters of this book, you remember that I said homeschooling is a lifestyle. In our family, that lifestyle includes random headache days for mom.

So here's how it works:

On normal days, we are productive. The kids have daily household chores to accomplish, and they do these immediately after breakfast (which I make most of the time). When chores are completed, the kids get about 30 minutes of free time, in which they might go play outside or do something fun indoors.

Now school begins. At the time of this writing, I'm still homeschooling three kids, ages 9, 12, and 14. The older two have a list of "book work," which is how we refer to their independent work. These are the subjects they can complete without any help from me. They include Bible reading, literature reading, cursive handwriting or copywork, grammar or vocabulary exercises, science, and sometimes math (depending on the lesson content). My youngest child is still mostly dependent on me for her lessons, so I begin with her while the older two work quietly on their own. All of this lasts one to two hours.

Next, we break for playtime and/or lunch. While the kids eat, I begin our history read-aloud. We use stacks of great books for history/geography/science/art/music studies, so we generally gather around the living room on couches, or occasionally at the dining table and study as a group. This will also last 1-2 hours.

Besides all of this, each kid has some form of kitchen cleaning duty, and they all know how to cook some basic meals. They often volunteer to make meals. In their free time, they play together outside, ride bikes, draw, play board games, solve Rubik's cubes, and play the Wii.

This is on a good day.

But on a migraine day? It's much more relaxed and basic. I still require the kids to complete their chores and independent work, and they get meals on their own. And the rest of the day is theirs to have free time. If I'm able to hang out in the living room, I will usually take advantage of a documentary, science video, or historical movie that ties in with our current studies. If I'm bedridden all day, I don't worry about educational videos.

Here's the raw truth and why it's so important to understand the first chapter of this book (*Rethinking School*). We are living life, as imperfect and unplanned as it can be. Education is very important, but so is flexibility, independence, and maturity. On the days that I cannot be the mother that I want to be, my kids are learning and growing in ways that no textbook can teach. They are gaining their academic education during real-life circumstances.

This independent learning is a process. It does not happen overnight. And the kids aren't always cheerful and willing little angels. Some migraine days are smooth, and others leave me with a lot of catching up to do upon recovery.

So on the good days, it's vital to work with them diligently, training, coaching, encouraging, and reminding them to stick to a routine and be responsible. *The payoff is huge.* While you think you are teaching your children to manage on a tough day, you are also providing an essential education in life skills. Do you know how many young adults don't have these very necessary skills today? "Adulting classes" are popular because of this. But your kids won't need those classes. So you can check "home economics" off your list.

Now, you might be thinking, "That's great, but what if I have young children who can't feed themselves or do independent schoolwork?"

Good question. I have been there, too. My oldest is 23 now, and, with 5 kids I can promise you that I have been through every stage.

With little ones, your focus on sick days is *survival*. It sounds harsh, but really, as a parent that's true with or without homeschooling! So, continue in survival mode. Don't worry about phonics lessons or ABCs or preschool workbooks. They can wait. They *will* wait. Concentrate on getting through the day with the children fed and safely supervised.

Through most of my parenting years with migraines, I have not had outside help on sick days, so I had to get creative. I kept juice boxes in the fridge and easily accessible lunches and snacks for little ones like string cheese, goldfish crackers, sliced fruit, lunchmeat, PBJ, and other quick foods. I relied on videos, puzzles, crayons, and Legos to keep the kids occupied on the floor next to me. The house was often a mess the next day, but that was part of my normal life, so I learned to plan for it. Remember, *relaxing your standards is key*.

Routine is vital

You may or may not be a structured person in your everyday life. But in this situation, a daily routine for your children will make all the difference. Train them now. Train them on the days you feel fine.

Choose a schedule that's workable for your children, no matter their age. Whether it's a simple, daily "to-do list" or a schedule with certain times to do certain tasks, begin setting the standard for them to follow. Write it down and post it where everyone can see it. Go over it together each day.

It takes time to adapt to a new routine, so take it slowly and be patient. Gentle reminders throughout the day, throughout the week, month after month will make all the difference. You will look back a year from now and be amazed.

If you have the benefit of a close friend or relative who is willing and available to help you during sick times, by all means let them help! Let them know your situation and talk about concrete things they can do. There is no shame in this. It's a blessing, so accept the help and be grateful!

That's what my friend Kimberly does. Let's read her story now.

How Kimberly Homeschools with MS

Kimberly has had multiple sclerosis for 25 years. Her children are 14, 12, and 11.

At their ages, they are mostly independent in their schooling. Kimberly teaches school by introducing the lessons each morning, makes sure there are no questions, and then "turns them loose."

They don't adhere to just one homeschool style; Kimberly describes it as "hodge-podge," or what I like to call "eclectic."

She says, *"I pull from everything. Every kid is different, so what works for my oldest does not work for my youngest. As far as my school year schedule, it's kind of year-round. I have to take breaks with my illness. Year-round schooling allows us to meet the state school attendance criteria and allows my body to rest."*

So how does her MS affect her family's homeschool?

Kimberly would love to say that it does not; however, that is not the case. She calls MS the "predictable, unpredictable disease."

"I can literally wake up in the morning and feel like I could run a marathon; however, by the time I brush my teeth fatigue has hit. So, it forces us to have a shell of a day. By that, I mean, we get the basics out of the way. This allows me to alleviate the self-appointed guilt I place on myself for having MS and not being able to homeschool my kids properly. If it gets really bad, I have to call my parents. Over the years, I have learned not to wait too long. One, it earns me a lecture from my dad. Secondly, my parents can establish a rhythm with the kids early. They can come in, check on me, make sure I am okay, and start the day with the kids. If not, they come in mid-morning. They have to not only worry about me, but they also have to

divert the kids focus from worrying about mom, to getting on with the school day."

I asked Kimberly what specific helps she has in place for sick days.

"My mom and dad are my home school help when I have a really bad day...or week...maybe two. My parents know where everything is located. They know the lesson plans. They know how to use the teacher's manual. It helps that my mom is a long-time educator so my kids can't pretend they don't know what to do. If not, then my dad will do what he calls "old school life skills" with them. And Viola! They remember what they are supposed to do! Something about learning to rotate the tires in the Texas heat, and it's a miracle! My oldest remembers he does know how to do his Algebra 2 homework. Go figure!

It also helps that my parents have a say in the curriculum. This is a huge help. That way, if they do need to step in for a prolonged period of time, they know what to do. They were there making the decision with me. Yes, it can get a little heated at the homeschool convention, because "I have been teaching for over 40 years. I have a Doctorate. I think I KNOW what is best for my grandchildren," gets a little old. However, after some prayer and silently seething under my breath, "Remember...final say in the retirement community mom..." Let me stop, I would never say that to my mom. Well, I may think it, but don't voice it. Not trying to get laid out on the convention floor by my mother. I still have a very healthy and respectful fear of my mom. Eventually, we manage to come to an agreement on something that everyone is comfortable with using. So, I can focus on healing and not explaining what is going on. I also put assignments in Google classroom. My parents are administrators as well. This one helps because they can review everything too and add comments on their work. It is just another set of eyes.

What tips or advice does Kimberly have for a homeschooling family with chronic illness?

"Write down your goals. Write down the goals you want for your family, each one of your kids, and more important, yourself. Moms, do not neglect yourself. Even if you have to sit in the closet and close your eyes for five minutes, do it. We are all scared; do not be afraid to ask for help.

Be bold when you tell people you homeschool your children. Oh, and maybe dial down the snark when you tell other people that you homeschool and get the classic response, "I could never homeschool.' You learn to nod, smile, and say, "It's not for everyone". Umm hmm, we all know this is the equivalent to 'bless your heart' in home school language.

I would also tell new homeschool moms that even though we have been homeschooling for (pick a number of years) we still get overwhelmed as well. Yes, there are times we want to throw out the entire curriculum and start again. So, what if you need to? Do it. Public schools do it, too. They just don't tell you.

Finally, embrace the journey... and boy, what a wonderful journey it is. Whenever you get stressed, sit down and look over your homeschool goals. Center yourself, breathe, and continue on your path."

I hope you're starting to notice a trend. Chronic illness brings its own struggles, whether it's repeated doctor appointments, reduced activity, or cancelling plans. Often, homeschooling helps to bring freedom from stress in circumstances that are otherwise very stressful with a traditional school upbringing. Whether the parent or the child suffers from an illness, the flexibility in homeschooling gives families the option to schedule their lives (and their schooling) as they need to.

How to begin

Write down how illness affects you and your family. Is it predictable or not? How old are your kids? What are their basic needs on a daily basis? What are they capable of doing without your help? Make a plan for these days (or whatever time frame you're dealing with).

If you need outside help, talk it over with that person (spouse, friend, relative). Make a plan for what your needs are, the children's needs, etc. Do you need a meal? Do you need a sitter? Do kids need a ride to lessons or part-time jobs?

If your kids are old enough for the family to be self-sufficient, make a written plan for them. Discuss meals and chores. Make sure there's something easy to cook (or sandwich fixings) or keep an extra casserole in the freezer. Talk about what absolutely needs to be done, and what the free-time options should be.

Do the kids know what they are allowed to do in their free time? What are the rules for electronics, TV, or outside play?

Adjust your school-year schedule so that these special times can be accounted for. Create a calendar year that works for your family and that meets your state's homeschool requirements. Make a list of the school assignments that your kids can complete without your help, or brainstorm other fun learning activities that can be done, such as puzzles, flash cards, videos, or reading.

Planning ahead and training for what you know is coming will give you peace of mind and will give your kids a feeling of security and purpose.

Whether you have a constant illness, occasional flare-ups, pregnancy bedrest, or something else, be encouraged that home education is still very much within your reach!

CHAPTER 8:
FROM TWO INCOMES TO ONE

"When you homeschool your children, you have to make sacrifices: of your time, of your energy, of your money. Speaking of money, you know, when I look back, living on one income all those years meant we didn't drive expensive cars or go on extended high-end vacations. But that wasn't important. What was important was that we had time together...nothing can replace that. You can have that time too. Concentrate on the positives, and enjoy your time with your kids. You won't be sorry."

-Barbara Frank

Ahh, we're back on the subject of money. In *Chapter 2* we discussed not being able to afford home education. In this chapter, I want to discuss the very real prospect of a family going from two full-time incomes to one.

This is a huge lifestyle change, but it's definitely doable. It requires an entirely new mindset, and quite possibly some big life changes.

First Things First

Obviously, budget is the main consideration here. If your household is used to two incomes, you will need to become a super sleuth in the cost-cutting department. I won't lie to you; this might be painful. You may find yourself being forced to reconsider some regular purchases that make you happy.

Before you do this, it is imperative to know your goals and your WHY. Your child's needs, your conviction about their education --- whatever your reason is for homeschooling, it needs to be solidified. Write it down. You (and your spouse) must understand the importance of this decision before you will be able to commit to the huge financial change on the horizon.

You can read more about this in Part 2. Take a day or two (or a week) and really work out your reasons. What led you to even consider this option? What is the need? Is it your child's current school situation? Is it a personal or spiritual conviction? Is it a family need? Whatever it is, write down what's on your mind. Write down your feelings, your child's feelings and circumstances, everything.

Because when you look at your new one-income budget and mournfully give up your daily latte, you'll want to have a vivid reminder of why you're here.

Budget Considerations

As a two-income family, there are very likely items in your budget that do not exist for one-income families where a parent stays home full time. Because one parent is going to be home full-time, certain things just aren't necessary, like:

- Lunches out
- Fast food suppers
- Dry cleaning
- Day care
- Work wardrobe
- Extra gasoline expense (depending on the commute)
- Union memberships
- Income taxes
- Hired housecleaning or lawn care

IF you currently have children attending public or private school, consider some of the cost savings by bringing them home:

- School uniforms
- Convenience foods for lunch
- Costs for extracurricular events

Now it's time for a little homework assignment. Take some time to calculate what you spend on these things per month. If you aren't even sure, start keeping your receipts today. Even better, do what my hubby and I occasionally do, and track every single dime spent by the family for a week or a month. Then take a hard look at what is necessary and what is not. It's a bit shocking if you've never done this!

But wait! There's more! When a parent is at home, there is more time to devote to other things that reduce the budget, like meal planning, cooking from scratch, house cleaning, lawn care, etc.

Additionally, you and the children will have the chance to get more sleep and live under less stress by not rushing out the door to separate locations early every morning. You will see your health improve with this very simple but profound change. There may very likely be a change in medical issues in your family.

Sonlight creator and homeschool mom, Sarita Holzman enlightens us on one very overlooked benefit of homeschooling:

"Homeschooling can definitely improve children's health. They often get more sleep, more active play, healthier food, and are exposed to far fewer germs. I also think homeschooling can be great for your *health as a parent. Much of that comes from the flexibility that homeschooling gives you to craft the lifestyle you want."*[12]

Sacrifices

"Oftentimes, the inability to afford to homeschool comes from a financial lifestyle that isn't conducive to living on a single income. Sometimes, the circumstances are beyond one's control (massive hospital bills, ongoing special needs care, loss of a home, etc.). In most cases, however, it is either that

a family has expectations of living "the American dream" and they won't make sacrifices necessary to ensure that they can live on one income, perhaps having one vehicle, forgoing cable television, or doing without eating out or going on expensive vacations." – Israel Wayne, Answers for Homeschooling[13]

Besides giving up expenses related to work and school, it may be necessary to dig even deeper into your financial situation to afford the homeschooling lifestyle. It may require a reduction in the type of spending you do on the fun stuff. OUCH. Yeah. Maybe your professional manicures or your daily specialty coffee will have to go. Maybe the vacations you take will need to be reduced?

This is where that written WHY comes in handy.

When you read the reasons for giving your child a specialty education in the safety and loving environment of your home, some of those extra things seem so much less important. Happy, healthy, well-adjusted children vs. perfectly beautiful fingernails? It's really not such a hard choice when you think about it.

Could you give up movie theater tickets and have a movie night at home with popcorn and homemade cookies? If you have daughters, could you have a fun "spa day" at home with them? If you have sons, could you trade tickets to a major league sporting event for shooting hoops together in the backyard? I think you could. Because you know something? Kids practically live and breathe on family time, not on expensive outings. A board game with parents is worth far more than dropping $75 at Chuck E. Cheese.

Even Bigger Sacrifices?

The fun stuff isn't the only hard thing to consider. Is your home or car costing you more than it should? Could you live with less? Could you sell a second car and trade it for something used? Could your house be downsized? Because that may be worth consideration.

A friend of mine once said, as she examined her large beautiful home, her baby in day care, and her teaching job, "We were working hard to afford a beautiful home that no one was home to enjoy, while someone else raised my baby so I could earn money to pay for the house that no one was home to enjoy." Kinda makes you think, doesn't it?

Do you see why knowing your WHY is so important?

Let me share a little something with you. My husband and I, with our five children, used to live in a little 960 square foot house. It had 3 tiny bedrooms, no dining room, 1 bathroom, and no laundry room. It was going to be temporary, and ended up lasting 5 years.

Do you know what my kids don't remember? The younger kids don't even remember how crowded it was. Why would they care? They had everything they needed! It was tough for me, but I learned many lessons there about contentment and patience.

We have given up some things, said no to some things, and done without many things. But anytime a lack of funds comes up, I remember what we have gained. We have enjoyed every minute of our children's childhood with them. We don't just spend Saturdays and Sundays and weekday evenings with them. We are a full-time family. We know what they're learning in every single subject. We are their main influence. THAT is priceless.

I asked some friends of mine to share about giving up their second income to homeschool. Here are their stories.

Misty and Robbie

Misty began homeschooling her son when he was in the third grade. She had been a fitness instructor at the local YMCA. She said it wasn't hard to quit her career because she looked forward to homeschooling. But there were some issues raised by the lack of funds at first.

"We had to budget pretty strictly. Holidays were stressful, because other family members didn't understand or respect our financial situation about exchanging gifts. My husband & I fought a lot about money too. It was VERY stressful for him."

I asked Misty if the cost of curriculum was a concern. She said it wasn't because there are so many options out there.

How did they make it work financially?

She says, *"We DID budget, but I also taught fitness classes & worked as a personal trainer a couple hours a day. Later, we started a family business that we worked together a few hours a week. The business later turned into a pretty good money maker that our son is going to take over in a couple of years."*

Even though Robbie felt the stress all the time, he never regretted the decision. Misty says, *"It was stressful for him because he worries about bills getting paid even when we DO have money. Back then, we didn't have much at all, so he spent a lot of time worrying. I think it's just his personality. He never asked me to quit homeschooling & go to work. He never even asked me to stop going on "field trips" or doing anything extra curricular. He just wanted me to stop buying new bath rugs & shower curtains. He doesn't regret the homeschooling at all. In fact, like I said, HE'S the one who wanted us to do it originally."*

Bethany

Bethany was a schoolteacher for two years. Her oldest child was in 2nd grade when they finally decided to take the leap and begin homeschooling.

"It was scary at first because it was an almost $40,000-a-year pay cut. My husband did not make a lot of money, so it was a complete leap of faith. God has shown up and provided every single month though. We have not ever gone without anything we need."

When I asked Bethany how they adjusted to their new situation, she replied, *"We began to make more things from scratch, cut out the extras from our grocery bill, stopped eating out all the time, etc. After a few years I began selling essential oils to help supplement our income. My husband worked side jobs until I made enough for him to only work one job."*

Faced with the cost of curriculum, Bethany has relied completely on God. *"I was concerned about it at first, but, in all honesty, I prayed about it, researched, and then realized that kids do not have to learn from one set curriculum. Every year we have done something different by using whatever the Lord has provided. One year we found everything we needed at Mardel on clearance. We just had a hodgepodge of different publishers. One year we found everything we needed at the Friends of the Library sale. One year we did it only with Time4learning. This year we started out with books from the library and then a family in our church gave us an almost brand new set of Alpha and Omega curriculum for free. God provides if we only trust Him."*

Bethany adds, *"I would say that this world is not getting better and we have a moral obligation to protect our children. We will never go wrong by creating a safe environment for our children to learn in. Just focus on the fact that what you are teaching your children, no matter how it looks, is most likely going to be far superior than what they would ever receive in public school. Trust the Lord to provide your needs and to also show you the way to teach your children. Don't be afraid to use resources! Google is my best friend at times and the public library is an excellent source as well."*

Jammy

Jammy has 2 teenagers and has educated them at home for 14 years.

She says it was her husband's idea to homeschool. "In 2005, he came home one day from work and announced, 'we need to homeschool our children.' And my immediate response was, 'you've got to stop listening to (James) Dobson!' Our kids were 4 and 2 at the time.

Before homeschooling, Jammy was a licensed Physical Therapist. When I asked her how hard it was to leave her career behind, she answered, "Once I had prayed through our decision and received peace from the Lord, it really wasn't that difficult."

How hard was it to reduce your household income?

Somehow we managed. We took the Financial Peace course by Dave Ramsey and worked out a budget.

How did you make adjustments to your budget to homeschool?

We basically followed the budgeting process using percentages as laid out by the Financial Peace course. Mainly, we reduced our overall budget. One thing that helped is that our vehicles were paid for.

Were homeschooling curriculum costs a concern?

Not really. We both had peace about the decision and just walked through the door that God opened for us.

It has always seemed to work out...God has been so good to us. (Maybe because we were obedient to His calling?

Would you do it differently, given the chance?

Absolutely not! It has been the BEST decision we have ever made...by far!

What encouragement or advice would you give a family that was in the same situation?

1. Be obedient to God's calling.

2. Wives- follow your husband's lead if he is a Godly husband. Your husband is the principal, lean on him when necessary.

3. Attend a homeschool conference. You are not alone in this journey. There are many women who have gone before you and blazed that trail, all with varying approaches (Charlotte mason, classical, unit study, traditional, etc...).

4. God has equipped you to homeschool your children, no one knows them better than you do. Love them and trust God.

5. Don't feel like you have to stick with one curriculum once you've decided "This is it!", especially in the elementary years. By the time your children get to junior high and high school, you will have a better grip on their learning style. Although, it does make it easier for transcripts to decide on a path and stick with it by the high school years, but it is not necessary. If a curriculum is not working and learning has become drudgery, change it!

6. Most important, pray continuously.

There are many similar stories like this. Could you be the next one?

CHAPTER 9:

DADS, GRANDPARENTS, AND OTHER FAMILY MEMBERS

What is most important and valuable about the home as a base for children's growth into the world is not that it is a better school than the schools, but that it isn't a school at all.

- John Holt

Life is full of unusual circumstances and personal choices. More often than you realize, families don't look average. This is what makes home education so wonderful. It's not just for a few people that fit in a certain box. It's an extension of parenting --- an extension of family life.

Some families don't operate like their neighbors. Sometimes kids are being raised by their grandparents. I imagine you know a family like this. Sometimes Mom works and Dad stays home with the kids. I imagine you know this kind of family, too. Maybe I'm describing *your* family now.

Do you see why this book is titled ANYONE Can Homeschool? It's because it's true.

Grandparents

I have not had the privilege of becoming a grandmother yet, but I understand it's even better than being a mom. That's what everyone tells me! One of the reasons is because you've learned a lot over the years, and you know just how quickly time flies. Grandparents tend to cherish the little things that a busy, tired mama just didn't really focus on.

And so grandparents make wonderful homeschool teachers. Whether by helping the child's parents or raising the child full time, the grandparent is well positioned to play a significant role in homeschooling.

Remember Chapter 7 on homeschooling with illnesses? Kimberly shared how her parents act as co-teachers. I recently spoke with a single mom who is ready to begin her homeschooling journey. Her job requires travel, so her mom is planning to be involved in the homeschool process with her.

If you're a grandparent, homeschooling is no different than if you were the parent. Whatever your circumstances (financial, children with special needs, etc.) the advice in this book applies to you.

Fathers

Though most homeschool families feature a mom as the teacher, it's not completely unheard of to see Dad teaching the kids. The dynamics are not important. Like I said above, the beauty of home education is that pretty much any situation fits. And a teaching father is no different.

In some situations, both parents are independently employed from home, but Dad is the primary teacher. In other homes, Mom has a great job, or Dad is a natural teacher. But Dad is still a parent, so nothing has changed.

I'd like you to meet Chad, who teaches his children at home.

Chad

Chad homeschools his twin sons (and has a preschool daughter, too). His wife works and Chad teaches about 95% of the school.

He admits, *"If you had asked either my wife or me prior to having kids if we would homeschool we both would've said, 'Absolutely not. Zero chance.' But after our boys were born we started to realize that at some point we were going to educate them. We didn't want to just make haphazard decisions on the fly about something that important. So, we figured we should put some thought into it. We started talking about what it was we wanted our boys to get from an education and then started to look for avenues that would give them those qualities.*

(Let me add that this is some of the best advice for everyone! Talk about what you want for your kids in education and in real life. See Part 2 for how to work through this.)

Chad remembers, *"We knew kids at our church from all different backgrounds - public school, private school, and homeschool. So, we started to ask ourselves, "Of the kids we know, who is getting the education we are looking for?" It was consistently the homeschooled kids who seemed the most mature and most prepared. Once we realized that, we started to look into the idea (very hesitantly at first - I had no idea how to make it happen).*

Shortly after that, I was in Chicago giving a speech [before homeschooling, Chad traveled and spoke on the Constitution] at a fairly large event. After I was done speaking, a 13-year-old girl came up to me to engage me about the content of my speech. I was impressed right away because what 13-year-old girl has enough confidence to initiate a conversation with an adult, let alone one with the authority of just having been on stage?! She had all the qualities I wanted to see in my boys: she was poised, confident, well spoken, respectful, and she had depth. She spoke to me about things that mattered - not just Justin Bieber and the Kardashians - and she had her own opinions. Despite all those qualities, she was completely normal and fun to talk to. So, after she was done talking with me, I went over to her mom and said, "Tell me how you did that." That girl was homeschooled. At that point, the decision was made."

I asked Chad, "Can you tell me a bit about your family dynamic? Who works, who teaches, any special schedule, etc.?"

"We don't really have anything special in our schedule. We do school in the morning and then they have their activities. The trick is getting everyone to all their practices and games, etc. People always say, "Oh, you homeschool? How do you get them socialized?" I tell them, getting these kids socialized isn't the problem. You should be asking, "How do you get your school in with all the socialization they do?" That's the trick."

Would he do it differently, given the chance?

"Clearly I made some mistakes along the way. I would love to go back and not buy a few curricula that didn't work out and things like that. But that's all part of the learning process.

Homeschooling my boys is probably the hardest thing I've ever done (although part of that comes from them being twins). However, I wouldn't change it. We are constantly having things happen where my wife and I look at each other and say, "And that's why we homeschool." There is no other method of teaching that would have allowed them to be at the level they are at currently. They are above grade level in basically every subject. The excel in every one of their activities, whether it's AWANA at church, baseball, or Tae Kwon Do. I'm trying hard to restrain myself from listing their accomplishments - as a homeschooler it's very validating to see how well they do and I have a slight problem with boasting about it.

Beyond that, one of our boys has a behavior issue that we've had to deal with. It's incredible the progress he has made in the last couple of years. His doctor told us specifically that if he wasn't homeschooled, the problem would have been so much worse.

These are the things that are so rewarding: being able to be there to guide them and help them through things and being able to ensure that my boys grow up to become men.

All that to say, yes, it's extremely hard. But I wouldn't change it for the world.

Chad, what encouragement or advice would you give a family that was in the same situation?

Every homeschool parent I talk to says they went through a period at the beginning when they thought that they couldn't do it. It is overwhelming when you look forward and realize that you alone are responsible for teaching them everything they need to know and preparing them for adulthood. But you are capable of more than you think. Those same parents I talk to always say the same thing. After a year or so they started to get the hang of it and realized they could do it.

That was my experience. In the summer before 2nd grade I was starting to have those thoughts, "Maybe I can't do this. Maybe I need to put them in school." It was shortly after that when the dam broke for me and all the information and ideas I needed started flooding in. Now I'm in a groove and I know what I need to do.

The other bit of advice - don't plan too far ahead. Don't worry about how you're going to do high school or do next year. That's when you get overwhelmed. Just plan this month. Then the next month. One step at a time.

In fact, I used to try to plan a month out and I can't even do that. My boys go at different paces than I expect in everything. Things I expect them to speed through cause them trouble and lessons I think are hard are nothing for them. So, I have a rough idea of what I would like to cover for the rest of this school year. But I plan week to week because I just can't know what to expect from them. If I try to do more than that I get overwhelmed and find that I just waste a ton of time. We go at their pace - not based on some book or whatever some academic says their pace should be. If they struggle with something we slow down until they get it. If they get something right away, we aren't going to waste time going over it six times because we're "supposed to." Our goal is to actually learn the lessons; we do what we have to do to make that happen.

One final thing I would add: what I love about homeschool is that I get to teach them things that matter. So many things that are important get overlooked in regular school. I am already teaching my boys about finance and investing. They know what a mortgage is and what inflation is. Those concepts are so much more important than half of what is in our schools, and yet they are absent. When a parent is deciding whether to homeschool, it's important to think of what areas you will need to supplement at home.

When we were just beginning to make our decision I was thinking of topics I wanted my boys to be solid in. They needed to get a financial education, character education, a foundation in the Bible, they should be fluent in Spanish, among other things. None of those things are taught in school. Well heck! If I'm going to do all that I might as well throw in some math and science while I'm at it and call it a day.

Grandparent Homeschooling

Vicki has been homeschooling her grandchildren for 6 years. They are now 15 and 17 years old. They began the homeschool journey as a result of bullying in school. Ariana (the youngest) spent her days in school either crying or disturbing class, and one time she just left class altogether.

When Vicki began homeschooling the kids, she had no idea what she was doing, so she joined an online school (K12), and Ariana flourished. She went from reading so poorly that it was painful to listen to and impossible to understand to reading with emotion and a great flow of words. That was just the first year!

Cory, the older brother, was doing well in school, but after some time he began to goof off, ignore his schoolwork, lied about it, and then failed classes. So, after trying many things, Cory began homeschooling for the one-on-one advantage.

After a year and a half of using K12, Vicki realized the kids were spending a lot of time learning to take the STAAR test (Texas) and less being educated, so they stopped using the program.

She says, *"While it turned out NOT to be what we needed in the end, it definitely was what we needed in the beginning to get us going. We now belong to a homeschool group, learn at our own pace, and don't use a "curriculum," but use what we find that we need at the time we need it."*

I asked Vicki what challenges she has and how she has faced them. *"A lot of self-doubt, as in 'What in the world do you think you are doing? You have a GED. What makes you think you can teach?' Then it occurred to me that just everyday life is learning, and what I don't know, we can all learn together. God had given me the strength on many, many days to continue on a path that I never chose but would never give up now. Once the shell shock was over, I can honestly say that I am loving this!!! The beauty of homeschooling where we are, is that you get to do it your way and in your time. You get to make it fit for you."*

Would she do it differently, given the chance? *"Absolutely! If we don't learn from our mistakes, then they were a waste of time. For one thing, I would be more organized."*

Vicki wants families in the same situation to be encouraged: *"Don't give up! Give it at least a year to make sure the emotional kinks are sort of worked through. Remember, these are kids we are dealing with and they aren't exactly the most stable of creatures, if you know what I mean. And if you are a grandparent raising your grandkids, then you have a whole different dynamic to deal with. Have fun and celebrate the successes, even if they might seem small to others. If you know how hard it was to do it, CELEBRATE! For them and for you! Take time off if your day is a disaster. Just stop and watch an educational movie, take a walk, check out a museum, bake a cake, write silly letters and pass them back and forth... you get the idea. Just stop and be with them. Some days they need that more. And so do you."*

Homeschooling is not a one-size-fits-all thing. It is tailor-made for you and your kids. Find what fits and walk away from the rest. It's okay to start using a lesson, curriculum, book, etc., and then realize it is NOT working for you and stop using it. This doesn't define you or them as a failure, it just means it wasn't meant for you. And don't let others tell YOU how to teach, if you haven't asked for their advice or opinions. Believe in you, believe in your kids, and most of all, remember that God has got this, as long as you keep Him at the top of the class.

CHAPTER 10: HOMESCHOOLING AN ONLY CHILD

Homeschoolers happily speak with more ease and poise because they don't fear adults as authority figures. Their authority figures were always their loving parents, teachers, and often their best friends; if your best friend is your teacher and authority figure, education is less stressful.

-Rebecca Devitt, "Why on Earth Homeschool"

Families with only one child (or one child left at home) may seem like the least likely to need encouragement or tips for homeschooling. But if you are one of these families already, you know that more is required of the parent.

In families with two or more children, the playmates are built-in. There's always another child to talk to, play with, and get attention from. But with an only child, the parents' attention is constantly needed. When you add in homeschooling, it can seem like some long, lonely days stretching out ahead for both the parent and the child.

Let me encourage you: one-on-one time with your only child is not a bad thing! You have a golden opportunity to have your child's undivided attention. You have the gift of mostly uninterrupted time!

The "only-kids" I know who are homeschooled are some of the most mature kids I have met, and that is, without a doubt, because they spend most of their time with adults. Embrace it!

Yes, there can be some drawbacks, most notably the tendency to get bored and lonely without other children. But this is something that's easily managed. I've interviewed some friends in this situation to find out how they make it work.

Christie

Christie is homeschooling her 13-year-old son. They have been on this journey for five years so far. Their biggest challenge? "Making sure they have things to do after school without it always being on a screen." To address this, they try to get involved with local groups consisting of kids the same age. She does find it a bit difficult the older he gets.

Christie says, "Homeschooling an only child has its difficulties for both mom and child. The first year was so hard on me because I was used to having some time alone during the day. When I pulled Lucas from public school in 2nd grade all of a sudden I had a shadow! After the first year though I hated when he left my side. We have become so close since we began homeschooling. For Lucas the challenge was learning that it's okay to be bored; having to come up with ways to entertain himself when I had things I needed to do."

Lisa

My friend Lisa has three children, but two are grown and in college and military, leaving her youngest son as an "only child" at home. She says one of the most common issues she faces with teaching one child is staying on schedule. (Oh my. This is my struggle with five!) She addresses this issue by being flexible with her day. This is, after all, one of the most beneficial parts of being a homeschooler: choosing your schedule and the flexibility of changing it when necessary! She has a plan for each day, but if something comes up in the morning, they just move schoolwork to the afternoon.

Lisa tells me that one of the best parts of schooling one child is the amount of one-on-one-time she can spend with him, making sure he understands his lessons. The personal instruction is huge! He is old enough now to do a lot of independent work, but she is right there to help when he gets stuck on something.

Her son enjoys extra-curricular activities that involve other friends, such as cooperative classes and field trips.

Since Lisa also has a part-time job, she tries to make sure that lessons get done in the morning or afternoon so she can work in the evenings (when

Dad is home). They follow a "normal" school calendar, taking a summer break like many people.

When I asked Lisa what she would share with moms who also work, she encourages, "It can be done! Homeschooling can be done at any time of day or night; that's what makes it so great!"

Every family is unique. And since you are a family, not a school, you can tailor your child's education around your family's needs. Get creative and seek out opportunities to get out with other families. Encourage hobbies! Get grandparents involved. Embrace the possibilities that a small family can provide while your child is growing up!

PART 2

HOW TO GET STARTED

Now that you know that ANYONE can do it, let's get down to the details...

CHAPTER 11:

READY, SET, NOW WHAT???

The biggest mistake new homeschooling parents make is going into it with an 'all or nothing' mentality. That's a lot of pressure for something you've never done before...

— Jacqueline Wilson, The Homeschool Super Freak

If you're convinced that you can do this homeschooling thing, congratulations! My job here is done! Have fun!

Ha! That would be cruel, wouldn't it? I'm not going to give you the pep-talk without the how-to.

Consider this second part of the book your checklist for getting started. I'm going to walk you through the steps to take, and it will require some homework on your part.

Step 1: Withdraw

If your child is already enrolled in a public school, you will need to submit a formal withdrawal. What this looks like can vary, depending on your state and the homeschooling laws. Homeschool Legal

Defense Association is a great place to start regarding state law (HSLDA.org).

Here are two options for withdrawal

1) Write a letter stating simply that your child will be attending school at home beginning on the date of withdrawal. You can either mail it (certified mail is best) or email it (CC the principle, teacher, and secretary). If your state has requirements for reporting or registration, include that information in your letter to the school. Check your local homeschool group for suggestions.
2) Go to the school in person and remove your child, pick up their belongings, ask for their school records or transcripts, and notify them of the withdrawal. Do this politely, no matter what your reasons are for the change.

How you do this will depend on many things, including the relationship you currently have with the school, your child's age/grade, and any other possible special situations.

Ask for confirmation that the school has received your notice. Otherwise, your child may be marked truant, which could result in legal issues.

You can withdraw your child in the middle of the school year if necessary by using this method. If it's summertime, depending on your district, you can simply skip the registration process for the upcoming year.

If you have moved to a new town or your child is too young to have attended school, you need not worry about withdrawal. However, since many states require some form of notification or registration (even to homeschool), check for those regulations first.

Step 2: De-school

This step is important for any child who has previously attended a public or private school. The purpose is to undo the school mindset, and for you and the child to start thinking in terms of home and family instead.

This step will be personal, depending on your family, the ages of your children, what their previous school experience was like, and your family circumstances. In fact, de-schooling will happen simultaneously with the remaining steps. It might take a couple of weeks or a few months.

In some cases, families begin homeschooling because of unhappy or unhealthy circumstances at school. Whether it was bullying, a learning disability, a staff problem, or something else negative, this child needs time to decompress, relax, sleep more, play more, and not think about school books. *This is very important after an unpleasant school experience.*

But it's also important for children who did not necessarily leave a bad environment, because homeschooling is not like public school. And this time gives both parent and child a chance to get used to a new way of life: being together all day every day, a new schedule, possibly new chores at home, and possibly more sibling interaction. And most of all, it helps to form a plan for how education will take place in *your* home.

Now, de-schooling doesn't have to mean (and shouldn't mean) 8 hours of cartoons or video games. There are some fun and productive things to do during this time. Here are just a few ideas:

- **Rest and play.** Kids who have been on a public or private school schedule will suddenly have ample free time and will most likely embrace the extra sleep time and play time. Let them. Sleep is vital for healthy growth, and play is extremely important for development.
- **Get out and have fun.** Visit parks, museums, movie theaters, shops, craft stores, and any other place you just haven't had time for. Set up field trips for yourselves (you can call just about any business and ask for a behind-the-scenes tour.) Go camping for a week. Take a vacation (homeschooler bonus: you can vacation anytime you want to, and from September to May the tourist sites are not crowded!)
- **Learn something new.** Brainstorm something you or your children would like to learn and go for it! Learn to bake pies, solve Rubik's cubes, grow grapes, paint like Bob Ross, or catch fish. Hire a teacher, search YouTube for how-to videos, go to the library, or ask grandparents for help. If your kids are not in the brainstorming mode, nudge them a little by exposing them to great ideas with books, videos, outings, visits with friends, etc.

- **Incorporate some learning.** Create your own "summer reading program" with a chart, stickers, and a prize to earn (even if it's not summer). Challenge the kids to memorize a certain set of math facts, and then reward them with an ice cream party. Do spelling bees, Bible drills, or geography quizzes once a week (let the kids know what to study, go to the library or download a learning app, and give them a certain amount of time to prepare).
- **Try a unit study.** This is a homeschool buzzword that means "pick a topic and turn it into a multi-faceted learning experience." Whether it's football, sewing, knights, or volcanoes, let your student immerse themselves in this topic with books, movies, documentaries, projects, field trips, and more. Just turn them loose and you'll be amazed at the many "subjects" that are incorporated into an experience like this. If you don't want to do the work yourself, a quick internet search for "unit studies" will give you more than you can imagine!

And you know, it's okay to let them play video games, too. Start to create a new normal for your kids. Ease them out of the school mindset and into the home education mindset slowly. Watch their behavior for clues. Every family will do this differently. Let them have a mini-break and then begin a new schedule.

Step 3: Assess

Some parents reading this book will be looking at their preschooler or 5-year-old and considering the homeschool journey. If that's you, you're starting at the perfect time! It's so easy to begin at the beginning!

Now is a good time to observe your child's interests and abilities. Preschoolers are an open book! So, pick up on what interests them, and use that to guide your preschool time. Let play be their curriculum, with fun story books, nursery rhymes, songs, and a few hands-on activities.

My oldest son was fascinated (or should I say obsessed) with dinosaurs as soon as he could talk. For YEARS, they dominated his thoughts and his conversation. So I used that to engage him in learning. He wanted to know all the names, all the facts, everything he could find out. I used books, toys, games, videos, and free printables online to satisfy his desire for information on dinosaurs while encouraging him to learn more.

It's a fun time! But let me share a word of caution: try to resist the urge to begin formal schooling with tiny tots. I know it's exciting and you want to begin homeschooling NOW, but little ones need lots of play. If you do any learning activities, let them be natural, and not forced. There will be plenty of time for structured lessons later.

Now, if your child has already begun schooling, you might be surprised to find out that simply continuing at their grade level isn't the best guide.

Remember Chapter 1: Rethinking School? Grade levels are a convenient tool to manage hundreds or thousands of kids in a school. And while that grade level may give you a starting point, let it be just that: the starting point. Your child may be proficient in math right up to his current grade, but slow in reading or writing. The opposite might also be true. So be willing to assess a few different things.

And this is going to depend largely on their current age. A first grader is still at the beginning of her education, but a 10th grader is already building a high school transcript. You're going to be treating these very differently. The first grader may need to sharpen her reading skills, but the 10th grader will need to consider graduation requirements.

There are several good ways to determine where your child stands in his academic career.

- School records: You should be able to request your child's most recent report cards and test results from the school they just left. These do not need to dictate your school year but can give you a place to begin understanding your student's strengths and weaknesses.
- Placement tests: Many homeschool curriculum companies have free placement tests on their websites to help parents determine the best place to begin. When researching curriculum, these are a great tool to take advantage of. My family uses one company for Math, another for writing, and yet another for grammar. So before I

ordered, I would simply try the placement test to give me some information.
- Do your own assessment: This sounds vague and difficult, but really, it's not. Take math, for instance: your child should know how to add (simple numbers and then very large numbers), then subtract (easy subtraction and also with borrowing), then multiply, then divide, and then learn to use all of these in fractions, decimals, percents, etc. You can easily figure out where your child is in math with some conversation.
- There are also state standardized tests available to homeschoolers. These can be a helpful guide in determining math, writing, and reading levels. Some are done online and some in group settings.
- Look at curriculum catalogs, websites, etc. As you will find, many of these homeschool curriculum vendors do not use grade levels, but they still have "levels." You can peruse their guides to see what is taught in the different levels and decide where your child fits in that particular curriculum.

You might choose to use one of these methods, or several of them, or none at all. It will really depend on you, your child, their age, and your previous involvement in their education.

And don't write off the review process! There are so many instances where a child did take a course but didn't really learn the concepts. If you need to restart a level, that's ok. Call it what it is: review.

If it's too easy and boring, you can ditch it, but if it's still challenging, it's perfectly fine to work through it.

High School

For a high schooler, you will be planning for the future, so I highly recommend a "counselor meeting" between you and your child. Sit down together with a notebook and pen and discuss the following:

- Previous courses – what they loved, liked, or hated, and why.
- Your state's requirements for graduation, if any – make a list of what has already been accomplished and what he or she still needs. This can be fun, like making a to-do list and checking off some already-completed tasks!
- After-graduation goals – will the child attend college, trade school, work full time, travel, etc.? What are her dreams and goals? What do you want for him her? This will determine some of what ends up on the final high school transcript, such as specific courses, life skills, SAT prep, volunteer hours, and more. Does he need advanced math courses or more writing skills?
- Your child's interests – does your daughter love horses? Does your son love electronics? YOU get to incorporate these things into their education, because homeschooling is all about the freedom

and flexibility! You get to tailor an education for each specific child, and the child should have some input!

Sit down and brainstorm these questions, and then give yourselves a few days to think, talk, plan, and revise. And don't be surprised if the high school plan evolves over a few years. Your child may have a suddenly new inspiration for their future, or you may discover a great course that you had not considered before. Make a plan and keep it flexible!

Finally, the most helpful assessment is just conversation with your child. Talk to them about what they like to do (in school and in their free time). Observe how they behave with schoolwork, what kind of books they pick up at the library (or whether they don't want to read at all), and what they choose to do with a whole day of free time. Ask them about their favorite subjects in school, or what they absolutely don't like. Ask them why they like or don't like them. Get them to talk about their interests and what they would like to learn if they could.

It's helpful (and fun) to include your child in the decisions when it comes to their education. That doesn't necessarily mean that they must have equal say in courses, curriculum, or schedules, but since homeschooling can be so incredibly personalized, it's important to take the individual student into consideration.

The next step in this process is research, and that deserves a chapter of its own. Continue the de-schooling process during this time.

CHAPTER 12:
CHOOSING A CURRICULUM

Commit your work to the Lord, and your plans will be established.

--Proverbs 16:3

Research

Now's your chance to plan your direction. With the information from Chapter 2 on learning styles and homeschooling methods, you've got a starting point. Your family's circumstances will help you determine which method sounds right for you.

Conventions

Check out a homeschool convention in your area. Spring is the most popular time for these, though there are usually some happening year round. This is one of the best ways to see almost all the curriculum that is available, in person, presented by the creators. Many state homeschooling organizations hold their own conventions, and there are several nationally known conventions, such as Great Homeschool Convention, Teach Them Diligently, and Wild and Free.

Most conventions have a vendor hall where you can see the curriculum laid out in front of you, flip through the books, ask questions, and purchase at a discount. There will also be workshops that are extremely valuable, with speakers on almost every topic you could want (from beginners to math tips to character training to college acceptance).

At these conventions, you will discover what most people don't know: the resources available to homeschoolers are almost endless. You have hundreds of options, and you'll see many of them all in one place at the large national conventions.

Most conventions are kid-friendly. I always enjoy bringing my kids along to these and they love it! They like to see the new games and books available, get a new t-shirt, and even give their input on a new curriculum. Many large conventions have activities for kids and teens to do while parents shop and sit in on workshops. Some kids, like mine, will enjoy perusing everything with Mom and Dad.

Visiting a convention may be overwhelming for the first time, but it is a wonderful way to jump in and learn all about your options, and the homeschool world in general. You will be amazed at the large community!

Further Curriculum Research

Next to conventions, the internet is your second-best option. Explore curriculum websites and read up on their products. Search out curriculum reviews by moms who have used those resources. Join and follow social media groups that allow you to ask questions and get input. The nice thing is that a convention website will usually have a long list of vendors (and links to their websites).

Oh, and social media? It's a homeschooler's BFF. Search out a few great homeschool bloggers that match your needs and interests. They'll often share reviews of curriculum, how-to's, great ideas, and freebie links.

Finally, talk to homeschoolers in your area. Ask them what they use, what they like, and why. Request an opportunity to look through their curriculum, teacher's guides, and projects they do. Find out how they use it, how much time the parent spends helping or if it's independent work, etc. Homeschool moms love to talk about what they use!

Teaching and Learning Styles

In Chapter 2 I outlined the different learning styles that children have, as well as the different homeschooling styles. These are just two areas to begin with, but there are others, too.

As I stated before, the homeschool curriculum world is huge. Really huge. One of my homeschool mom friends, who was a public school teacher before, told me that she was absolutely amazed at the wide variety of resources available to her when she began teaching her own children. Choices abound for every family size, every ability, every budget, and every interest.

How to Choose

First, don't make this step harder than it must be. There are so many amazing options that you can get overwhelmed. But take it in small bites, and start where you are right now. Start with core subjects like reading, writing, and math. Remember the 3 Rs? There's a reason for this. These are essential for all other knowledge, so every child must master them.

It's acceptable (and recommended) to begin your first year just doing these basics and getting comfortable there. Round out the learning with lots of stories and field trips. Once you've settled into a routine with curriculum that works, then consider expanding your subjects list. Find a great way to incorporate history and science on a level that is possible at your house.

Trust me: trying to dive into seven subjects a day, for five days a week will result in tears, burnout, and frustration for a first-time homeschooler. Start slow and then add more as you feel ready. If you have state regulations, start with the minimum!

After you've assessed a starting point for your children, consider your budget. This is often one of the biggest concerns, as Part 1 has already addressed. How much are you willing or able to spend on school curriculum? How much is too much?

Next, think about the subject that you might want the most "help" with. If you're unsure how to help with math, start with that subject and find a program that has video instruction, online resources, or a detailed instructor's guide. Do the same if you have a beginning reader and are unsure how to approach phonics.

If you've researched the homeschooling styles in Part 1 and are leaning toward a certain method, your search will be easier. For instance, if you've chosen a Charlotte Mason style, your search will be narrowed quite a bit. If traditional schooling is more comfortable to you, a boxed curriculum from one company just may simplify your purchase.

Since this book largely addresses out-of-the-ordinary circumstances, you will definitely want to figure in these issues when buying: special needs, work schedules, cost, outside help, and more.

With all this in mind, your planning may look like this:

a) If budget is the main concern, you'll want to start with your spending limit. If you're also a working mom, you'll need to figure in your work schedule and how that affects the kids. A curriculum that is 1) on budget and 2) can be used independently by your children narrows down your options.
b) If your qualifications as a teacher are the main concern, you will want to search for a

curriculum that gives you lots of structure and guidance. Maybe it's a traditional curriculum with full teacher's guides, video supplementation, or live online classes.
c) If your child has special needs, you'll put these needs at the top of the list. But like my friend, Tiffany, if you have a part-time job, your plans will need to revolve around your daily schedule.

Mixing Resources

You can absolutely mix and match to suit your child's needs. For example, math worksheets, instructional videos, and online games can all be combined to provide a wonderful math education.

Many families choose their curriculum from a variety of companies and internet sites, while others purchase everything from one curriculum publisher. The entire point of this book is to *do what works best* for your family, and that sometimes includes purchasing curriculum from a variety of sources.

While one company may have an amazing language arts program, you may be less enthused about their math offering. That's okay, and it's pretty normal. That's exactly what makes homeschooling so wonderful: the freedom and flexibility it allows.

Taking Charge

Along these same lines, don't become a slave to the curriculum. Use your parenting instincts. Be flexible and observant.

This is often scary for beginning homeschool parents because, as I mentioned in beginning chapters, we have been trained to believe that parents don't know much about education. But you do know a lot about your child, and you are going to continue to grow in that expertise.

If a curriculum is great but there is too much busywork, reduce the work required of your child. If there is too much reading or writing for your child, you absolutely have the power to adjust that. Whether it's the "calendar" provided or the speed of progression, you can and should make choices along the way that are best for your child.

And sometimes that might mean that you ditch a particular curriculum and try something different. That can be a little painful. When we invest time or money into something, we really want it to work. It's okay to let it go, though, and find something better. Sometimes you don't know what will work *until* you try it.

What else will you need? Pencils, paper, crayons or colored pencils, scissors, glue, and access to a library and the internet. Start with the basics and then expand as you see fit. If you don't have internet access at home, schedule library access, and budget a certain amount of money to print pages there. Take advantage of online book reservations at your library (or several libraries in your area) and use interlibrary loan for the books they don't have.

Home education is personal and flexible. Don't despair if it doesn't look like what you imagined. Start with what you have. You can do this!

CHATPER 13: THE STRUGGLE IS REAL

Everyone thinks it goes smoothly in everyone else's house, and theirs is the only place that has problems. I'll let you in on a secret about teaching: there is no place in the world where it rolls along smoothly without problems. Only in articles and books can that happen.

- Ruth Beechick

I've spent this entire book telling you that anyone CAN homeschool, so now I'm going to share some brutal truths with you. I wouldn't be doing you any favors by making you believe it's all sunshine and roses.

Homeschooling has its ups and downs, because it's an extension of parenting. If your kids get tired and cranky under normal circumstances, you can bet they will do the same during school time. If they disobey or outright defy you in regular life, they will absolutely do so during lessons. If you get tired and impatient as a parent, you will also face this as the teacher.

So, let's be honest. You're becoming the most full-time of full-time parents, and your resilience is more necessary than ever.

Math lessons make some kids cry. (Math lessons make some parents cry. Ask me how I know!) Handwriting practice will try the patience of an otherwise pleasant child. Getting out of bed to do schoolwork instead of sleeping til noon and playing video games might just bring out the monster in your teenage son.

Kids are kids.

Just because you're excited about this new journey and have grand plans and schemes does not mean that your children will naturally adopt your enthusiasm. They may feel a little excitement about a new thing, or they may be more excited than you --- at first. However, getting down to the actual process of school with Mom or Dad will lose its appeal for some kids, and the normal childhood behavior will surface.

Don't panic. And don't assume that your homeschool is a failure. Because it's not.

I've seen and heard from so many moms who think that because there are tears or disobedience, they cannot teach their child at home. They have forgotten all the reasons they chose homeschooling and let a bad day or a behavior problem take away their convictions. They give up and send their child back to public school.

But, think about this: will behaviors improve at school? Will the underlying problems be solved? The short answer is NO. Behavior issues are behavior issues, no matter where the kids are.

It's common when you tell someone you're homeschooling, to hear a parent proclaim, "I could never spend all day with my kids!" It's probably because they have not taken the time to teach character and discipline. They have created little monsters and don't want to deal with them.

Don't be those parents.

The truth is character is so much more important than today's math lesson. It's imperative that your child learns proper behavior, whether it's obedience to parents, working hard until a task is complete, being patient, and the list goes on.

So, what do you do?

If a behavior problem arises during school, stop what you and the children are doing and address the problem. This is parenting. Identify the problem (in love), state the expected behavior, and hug. If necessary, move on from the schoolwork and take a walk or an early lunch break. Inform the child(ren) that, "We will try again tomorrow." And tomorrow, begin the school day with a gentle reminder of the behavior issue and the requirements (again, in love).

If character training has been missing in your home, now is a great time to include it. In fact, it may be a perfect way to start your school morning.

I really love *Our 24 Family Ways* by Clay and Sally Clarkson.

Now, don't assume it's only the kids who have some adjustments to make. Everything I just described can also affect the homeschooling parent.

Trust me, to deliberately train your children all day, through chores, schoolwork, and sibling relations, takes stamina. And maybe some caffeine and quiet time. And most of all, the grace of God.

When your sweet little daughter suddenly turns grouchy during phonics, or your son complains loudly that, "This math is taking forEVER!" you will likely ask yourself how you ever got talked into this! What were you thinking??

Dear moms and dads, just remember that this could be green beans at dinner or picking up the mess in their room. The strong will is there, but it can be tamed. And it is worth your time. It is worth your patience. It is worth digging deep down inside yourself for that unconditional love of a parent.

You are changing their childhood and you are changing your family. It is a process. It's full-time parenting. And it's worth every minute, every discipline session, every tear, and every hug.

What Will My Friends Say?

If you are in a circle of people where homeschooling is basically non-existent, you can expect to get lots of questions, and maybe even some unfriendly and uncaring responses.

Sally Clarkson, in her book *Seasons of a Mother's Heart*, says:

The decision to homeschool will, by its nature, create division. To those who choose to put their children in public school, your decision to homeschool is a passive condemnation of their lifestyle. Since homeschooling rejects the educational status quo, it invites criticism and rejection, not just for us as adults but also for our children. Family members, church members, friends, and even strangers will question your decision and scrutinize your life. I am finding that only heart-deep dedication and sacrifice enables me to confidently say, 'This is right...this is what God wants me to do...this is worth it.' Because I know that doing God's will is worth whatever the cost may be.[14]

Be strong in your conviction that this is best for your family. Bring up your WHY. Share it with love. And then go on with your homeschooling. You've put a lot of thought, consideration, research, and time into this lifestyle, and it won't appeal to everyone. That's okay. Maybe your favorite brussels sprouts recipe doesn't appeal to everyone either, but you don't have to stop making it, right?

There may be some negative comments; maybe even some hateful ones. Often, these are the result of ignorance. People who have never actually homeschooled or witnessed a homeschool day or been close friends with a homeschool family usually criticize from a point of *just not knowing*. So don't let them discourage you or talk you out of it. They don't live at your house, or know your needs, or have your convictions. They just don't know.

Avoiding Burnout

As I said, you are becoming the most full-time of full-time parents. Prepare for an adjustment period. And prepare to hit a period of burnout.

If you're super-excited to begin this venture, you may be squinting your eye at me right now, thinking it's just not possible to burnout! And maybe it won't happen to you at all, or not for a long time. But I want you to be aware of it: the signs, the causes, and the solution.

The cause can be obvious: you're devoting your time to the complete upbringing of one or more children. Combining the running of a household with the new addition of educating children can make you tired, frustrated, or overwhelmed. Just know: this is normal! Parenthood is a big job! Don't give up; just take a breather.

James Dobson famously said, *"Raising children is the most important job in the universe."* It is important, and that's why it's such a big deal. Nothing worth doing is ever easy!

So what should you do when you start to feel burnout?

Just what you'd do in any other situation. Take a break. Change things up. Have a little fun. Try something new.

In homeschooling, that might mean taking a week off. For me, that's always been what helped. Just a fun break from the schedule, sleeping in, movies and snacks, trips to the lake, or other activities. Or maybe it means changing up your school routine. Could you rearrange some of your daily tasks, or your weekly schedule?

When you are parent, household manager, wage earner, and teacher, life can get overwhelming. It's okay to take a break wherever you can, whether it's to breathe, reassess, or make changes.

Don't confuse burnout for the feeling of "I can't do this." Recognize that we all feel this in many areas of life. Stop and assess, and then come back strong.

CHAPTER 14:
THE LAW

Any society that would give up a little liberty to gain a little security will deserve neither and lose both.

-Benjamin Franklin

In the United States, it is 100% legal to educate your own children. There is not a federal law, but each state has its own rules. They range from states with no requirements to states that require annual reporting, annual test submissions, and oversight from the local school district.

It's very important to learn which laws you'll be under before you begin. You will want to follow your state's requirements closely from planning to implementation.

There is a national homeschool organization called Homeschool Legal Defense Association

(HSLDA), and it's the first place I recommend checking for your state's homeschool laws. In addition, it's a great starting place for information about state organizations. A state organization is more closely involved with your state's laws and homeschool history.

Now, don't panic if you feel like your state has some strict oversight, but a relaxed homeschooling method seems to fit your family best. There are experienced parents in each state who can help new homeschoolers navigate the requirements. This is why finding a state organization and local support is so important.

I want to encourage you, no matter where you're going to be homeschooling, to follow the law. Don't ignore it. The freedom to educate our children at home is such a basic parental right that we do not want to jeopardize it. If your state requires yearly testing, do it. If your state requires monthly visits with a district representative, do it gladly and welcome the rep with kindness and enthusiasm. If your state does not have requirements, do a little happy dance and get started planning!

My Story

At 7:00 one morning in October 1983, police officers knocked on our door in Terral, Oklahoma. I was 11 years old, and we had been homeschooling for just about one month.

A very apologetic deputy informed my parents that they were under arrest for truancy. He was there to take them to the County Sheriff's office.

My parents immediately called our pastor, who went to inform my aunt Kari (she also homeschooled her children), who lived across town, that the deputy was on his way to her house, since she didn't have a phone. The pastor's wife volunteered to keep all four of us kids, (my sister and I and our two young cousins) and the pastor drove my parents and aunt to the jail.

Mom and Daddy were members of Home School Legal Defense Association, so phone calls were quickly made. John Eidsmoe, who was a professor of law at Oral Roberts University at the time, took my aunt's case at no charge, since she was a widow.

The legalities of homeschooling were a big deal at this time, as homeschooling had begun to grow in popularity. At the time, there were 7 homeschool defense attorneys in Texas. But no one expected a problem in Oklahoma. Oklahoma was, and still is, one of the best states for homeschooling, so this was unheard of!

My Dad worked for the County Sheriff's office. He had been there for about 6 months when he was suddenly fired without warning and without explanation just three days before.

Bail was set for $200, which our pastor graciously paid. So, Mom, Daddy, and my aunt were fingerprinted and processed, but never locked up. They spent the whole day sitting in the Sheriff's office while the attorneys were contacted.

The court date was set for January of 1984. In the meantime, John Whitehead called the Oklahoma

Attorney General and the State Legislature. My aunt got a phone at her house in order to keep up with the case. We visited with the attorneys handling the case. All of the children were questioned privately to prepare us for the court proceedings.

In December, my aunt received a phone call from another Oklahoma homeschooler who said that 300 other homeschoolers were planning to march at the courthouse where the case would be heard. She was so happy just to know there were other families who homeschooled in Oklahoma!

Just days before the case was to be tried in court, the Terral School Superintendent dropped the case. He even came to our home and apologized to my parents for the inconvenience.

I was eleven and my sister was eight, and my cousins were seven and four. What I remember is the fear of having police officers knock on our door so early in the morning, and finding out that they had come for my parents.

I remember spending the day at the pastor's house, waiting for my parents to come home. I did have some worry that they might have to stay in jail. We had only been homeschooling for just over a month, so it was scary to think they had done something really wrong.

I'll never forget that homeschool freedom is precious and fragile.

As far as my Dad recalled, our families were the first to be arrested for homeschooling in Oklahoma. There are many families who have been through a similar ordeal, or worse. Thanks to the hard work of homeschool pioneers, and state and national organizations, all parents in America have the legal right to educate their children at home.

These days, homeschooling is very popular, and problems with authorities are very unlikely. However, we must be good stewards of the freedom we have.

Protecting the Freedom to Homeschool

This book is based on the idea that homeschooling is an extension of parenting, and as such, is a basic right of humans. However, various governments and numerous average citizens do not necessarily agree. There is a very common mindset that parenting is best assisted with government help and that parents cannot be trusted to completely oversee the raising of their children.

You'll quickly learn that the freedom to homeschool is always in jeopardy. It's only been a common legal practice since the 1980s. So, there are two things a homeschooling parent must do:

1) provide a proper education for their child along their state's guidelines

2) keep an eye on any legislation that would limit that freedom

If you're in a state that has multiple requirements, you need to be the most vigilant, because the gradual encroachment of freedom is already underway. If you're in a state with complete freedom (like me), it's important to protect it by having a good relationship with your legislators and encouraging them to vote "no" on any bills that might arise to limit that freedom.

Vouchers

I believe that school vouchers used for homeschooling are an encroachment on freedom. As currently proposed in most states, they allow a parent to "use their tax dollars" to pay for private school or for homeschool curriculum. This sounds great on the surface, but beware! These vouchers will come with strings, as they should. Every tax dollar spent should meet general requirements and should be answered for. Vouchers will be no different.

As you are already aware, tax dollars spent on anything religious results in cries of "separation of church and state" (despite this being an erroneous statement). If the non-religious requirement is not there in the beginning, it will change because of public dissent.

Vouchers will (and do) have lists of approved curriculum. This might sound like no big deal, until you have chosen a curriculum perfect for your family, only to find that it is not on "the list." So, then you'll be forced to choose between the best and the approved. This is a loss of freedom.

But that's not all. Using tax dollars for private and home education is like using tax dollars for public education. It all boils down to government-funded, public education, otherwise known as public school. Voucher recipients will be (and are) subjected to the same rules as public schools.

If you have chosen to leave the public school system, why on earth would you want to submit to it at home? Whatever your reason for leaving, coming right back under that system is not the answer. It is not freedom.

I urge you to fight the voucher system in your state. If it already exists, don't take the bait. Bait is what it is. There is no such thing as "free."

Public School Participation

A very similar danger to homeschool freedom is participation in some public school activities, namely sports. These laws are commonly called "Tebow bills" because they copy the method that Tim Tebow, a homeschooled student in Florida, used to access sports as a student. Though schooling at home, he participated in sports at his local public school.

In states with no requirements or oversight, these bills are a first "foot in the door." Though they may not be originally written with testing or academic requirements, they will end up there. That's what's happening in Texas currently, as this (still failed) bill has evolved from a "no requirements" bill to a "testing-requirements" bill.

Isn't it a choice? If you don't want to use it, you don't have to, right?

This is a common argument, but look at it this way: homeschoolers are already under a microscope, because too many people still believe that parents can't possibly teach their own kids. The slippery slope begins here.

The danger in both vouchers and public school partnerships is the scrutiny of the entire homeschool community. As shown throughout this book, homeschoolers look very different from house to house, and do not follow any single kind of standard. One family will look very different from the next. This is not right or wrong, and families cannot be judged by every other homeschooler out there.

But that's exactly the danger. Because one person's neighbor receives a voucher or participates in the local school football program, and they have a non-traditional schooling, the neighborhood, the local ISD, the superintendent, and the state will begin to judge all homeschoolers based on those who are unfamiliar or misunderstood. Cries for oversight and compliance with new laws will begin. I know this because it happens already.

It is not worth the "free money" or the opportunity to play sports.

I've already addressed the cost of homeschooling in two separate chapters. Where there's a will, there's a way. And the way is always free when you commit to using your own resources.

If sports are an extremely important part of high school for your family, find or start a homeschool league in your area. They are everywhere, and they were all started by a homeschool mom or dad who felt the way you do. In case you didn't know, there are homeschool sports, bands, science teams, debate teams, robotics teams, and just about every other team activity you can think of.

Home Health Visits

This is a real and growing threat. Because of a handful of cases of child abuse among homeschool families (some were actual homeschool families and some were merely truant), there is a cry for home health and wellness visits for homeschool families.

This is not wise, and it is not freedom. Surveys have shown clearly that children educated at home are far less likely to suffer from abuse than their public schooled counterparts. The very random horror stories that come up in the news are not indicators of homeschool safety and should not be judged as such.

Watch your state legislature closely. Stay informed and defeat bills like this.

Homeschooling is a parental rights issue. Don't live in fear but do stay informed and vigilant. The pioneers of the homeschool movement have paved the way for you to do this; don't trade those rights for some government freebies.

Chapter 15:

How to Get Started

There isn't a right way to become educated; there are as many ways as there are fingerprints.

-John Taylor Gatto

If you're ready to begin, let's get down to the details.

Set Goals

For success in any endeavor, goal-setting is a must. Undertaking your child's education is no different. You'll have some short-term goals and some long-term goals. And don't be surprised if these goals change and evolve over time.

We have just discussed the process of planning your short-term goals in the previous section. De-schooling and research will have you well on your way. This will give you a pretty good idea of where you want to start and what your first year will look like.

Your short-term goals will be very specific to your children: teach a child to subtract, improve handwriting, review fractions, or improve sentence structure. Addressing shortfalls in the basics is a good place to start. Students always need to review and then build on the Three R's.

Then make time for the meaty stuff. History, geography, science, and literature all play an important role in a good education. Determine what's important for your children right now and don't stress about including it all in your first year. State history? High school biology? States and capitals? Focus on one or two that are both important and manageable this year. Jot the others down for future exploration.

Don't have a specific need in mind yet? Begin with something your child is interested in. Maybe he wants to read all about cowboys and Indians. Go for it! Maybe she is a math whiz. Look up famous mathematicians in history and start there.

A piece of advice: your short-term goals should include some non-school options, such as time management, discipline, and character training. Don't laugh! You'll begin to understand when you begin spending everyday with children who have previously been under the care of someone else.

Now for the long-term goals. This list will include your hopes, dreams, and desires for your children. This is a fun and easy list to create, and you will want to add to it as the days and weeks and years go by.

The long-term goals include everything from the core subjects in school to the character traits you want to see in your children. What kind of adult should they become? Well-read? Handy with tools? Confident public speakers? Frugal shoppers? Charitable? All of the above?

Do you have certain things you want your sons to learn and different things for your daughters? Is there a family business or recreational activity that they can learn to be part of? Do you want them to go to college or perhaps explore entrepreneurial opportunities?

Thinking through these questions is a great exercise in parenting, and it specifically directs your home education plans. With these answers in mind, a parent may view the big picture with hope and excitement, and then begin to determine the steps to take to help their child achieve them.

And as your children grow, you will begin to include their own hopes and dreams into the list of goals. You'll see their talents and gifts start to blossom. Their interests will guide you into new areas you may not have even considered.

Basically, you're the school counselor.

Your end goal is to send a well-rounded adult into the world. So much of what is going to be on this list of goals is considered "life skills" or "home ec" in the wider sphere of education. Before parents abdicated educational responsibility, it was just plain ol' parenting.

Kids can learn to count money, spend wisely, keep a budget, manage a checking account, and do their own taxes without a course in "adulting." They can learn to boil eggs or plan and cook an entire dinner for the family simply by casual training and daily observation. Your children can learn to debate a variety of topics in the safety and comfort of home, among people who love them and can gently prod them to see all sides of an issue.

Finally, let these goals be your guide, but not your master. We set goals to give us direction, but not to beat us down if we miss the mark. Be flexible.

Remember, the focus of this entire book is homeschooling *despite* the circumstances in which we find ourselves.

If your circumstances change, allow your list to change. Postpone some plans, rearrange your schedule, seek out different materials. And most important, let home education be the thing that teaches your children how to learn. When they know how to learn, a schedule change or a budget crunch or a life crisis will not prevent them from learning anything they want to know.

Schedules

If you've read this far, you'll know that there is not one right way to have a school schedule in homeschooling. Your family is unique and your schedule will be, too. But it's good to have one or at least a loose plan.

Whether you have a Monday-through-Friday plan, with lessons from 9 a.m. to 1 p.m., or you school in the evenings or Wednesday through Saturday, or have Grandma come on Mondays and co-op classes on Thursdays, write it all down. Will there be a music lesson, karate, or library visits? Do you want the kids to do certain chores each day? Pencil in your ideas, and then try this schedule for a couple of weeks. If something's not working, adjust.

There's so much flexibility in home education!

One of my favorite books for this process is *Managers of Their Homes* by Steve and Teri Maxwell. It gives you an easy-to-follow method for deciding what each member of the family needs to do and when to schedule it. Another great one (no matter your family size) is *Large Family Logistics* by Kim Brenneman.

Don't worry about how many hours the public school kids are away; don't set your clock by the neighborhood school bus. Determine how much time YOU need for your child's personalized education and be confident. If you get stuck on the public school mindset, go back and read Chapter 1 again.

Local Support

I highly encourage you to seek out a local group of homeschoolers. The variety is amazing, especially if you live in or near a larger city. There are groups for religious and secular families, special needs families, unschoolers, and more. Some groups are completely social and others are completely academic. Some are a mix of everything. Attend meetings, field trips, or other social events, and ask if you might visit their co-op for a day.

There are also some wonderful online groups, social media groups, and blogs where you can glean support, information, and inspiration. You'll be able to read about different styles, curriculum reviews, encouragement for hard days, buying and selling used curriculum, and just about everything else.

Just don't let the online world be your only support. It's a wonderful 21st century addition, but nothing beats face-to-face relationships.

Test every new idea or piece of advice against your common sense. Even in the homeschool world, there are trends, "celebrities," and cool kids. You may think you're the only one on the planet not using that popular new math curriculum or method or weekly circle time, and that's okay. If it's wildly popular but it's not for you *then move on*. I have never done poetry teatime, even though it seems to be what everyone on Instagram is doing.

Be realistic about your home and family and don't let trends push you all over the place. If you've found a great curriculum that no one else is using, it's okay to do a little reading and research. But at the end of the day, if it's working for you, there's no need to give it up.

Socialization

Oh, there's *that* word. It's common to hear it as a homeschooler, and it's apparently common to worry about it as a non-homeschooler. You may have worried about it yourself! Trust me: this is not a problem.

Socialization is simply the ability and the opportunity to interact with people. It should not mean just interacting with twenty-five kids of the same age. It means conversation, eye contact, manners, respect, and having fun with people of all ages. This happens naturally in the real world, and your kids will not lack for it.

If you attend a co-op, a club or sport activity, music lessons, church and youth events, trips to the grocery store, community involvement like 4H and Meals on Wheels...well, you get the idea. The average homeschool kid receives a more well-rounded social life because they are not bound to a classroom setting with only kids their own age all day.

My one caution: don't sign up for too many things the first school year. It's easy to get excited about all the possibilities, but you may find yourself quickly overwhelmed by the time commitments and possible homework requirements. Pick one or two things that fit your family and try them.

Ready, Set, Begin!

The day has come. You're all set up with curriculum, pencils, activities, a schedule, and high hopes. You are beginning a life-changing journey; for you, for your children, for your family.

Remember: **YOU ARE NOT A SCHOOL.** You are a parent. You can do this.

Pray. God gave you these children and the ability to raise them fully.

Start easy. Lay out the expectations you have for your children. And go easy on yourself and the kids. Work according to the plan you have written out but be flexible. Remember that you're dealing with humans here, and that involves a lot of flexibility and patience. If the first day feels long and overwhelming, it's okay to stop early. Pick up where you left off tomorrow.

Keep track of what you're doing (in some states this is a requirement). Write notes in a planner or in a simple notebook about what you accomplished. Jot down what you observe in your children academically, physically, and emotionally. If for no other reason, this will be a huge boost to your confidence to see what was achieved! We tend to focus on the negative, so this simple exercise will adjust your thinking. At the end of the first week and the first month and the first year, you will be glad you did this!

There will be hard days. Don't let those discourage you. Take a deep breath, figure out what's wrong, address the problem, and move forward.

CHAPTER 16:
ENCOURAGEMENT FOR THE LONG RUN

When the atmosphere encourages learning, the learning is inevitable.

-Elizabeth Foss

As you travel this new path of home education, you may face occasional doubts along the way. That's normal. After all, if you're reading this book, you're likely trying to do something new amid already trying circumstances.

You'll wonder if you're doing it right or if you're going to ruin your kids. Don't panic; most parents wonder this!

I'm here to address some of those doubts and fears before you are assailed by them.

There is no such thing as "behind" in homeschooling

This topic is one of the most popular posts on my blog. It's so common to worry about "getting behind" because we have been trained to think in terms of grade levels, test scores, and benchmarks. Once you become your child's teacher, you may find yourself comparing him to the other kids in the neighborhood, at church, or in your homeschool group.

Please. Don't.

Children were never meant to progress steadily up the same ladder at the same time like little robots. They are unique individuals with hearts, minds, and souls of their own.

The most unnatural thing in the world is to expect all nine-year-olds to learn multiplication at the same rate or all twelve-year-olds to understand algebra. Some will be math whizzes, and some will need lots of extra time and practice.

Some kids will read at four years old (two of mine did) and other kids will finally read at 8 (three of mine did). But guess what? They all read well and enjoy it.

I understand the comparison and the worry. I have been there. I was not so confident in my early years of homeschooling. But looking back on 20 years (and two graduates so far), I can promise you that, whether children learn quickly or slowly, they still learn. And by the time they finish school, they are all pretty much even with each other.

Your job is to encourage a steady progression. Help your child conquer the difficult things and encourage them to move forward in what they love. You'll find that, while they might be slower in one subject, there will be another subject that's a breeze for them. Let them slow down where they need to and let them move quickly in other areas.

Grade levels don't really matter

On that same note, let me encourage you not to get hung up on grade levels. These are another mass-schooling idea and not always applicable to home education.

It's an inside joke among homeschoolers that many don't even know what grade they are in. (It's true!) Your daughter can be in a math book meant for 3rd grade while excelling in 5th grade English. There are so many different scenarios like this.

That's why grade levels don't really matter. I like to think of them more as "progression levels," like in a video game. If you complete the first level, you're ready to move on to the next one. Your kids will probably love this analogy!

This is where home education is so beneficial to the student. They can spend the amount of time they need to master each subject, despite what every other kid their age is doing. Education is tailored to the student, and not the class.

If you're concerned about meeting standards, or if your state requires it, set goals. Make sure you keep working toward that goal with your child. Give them extra drill or practice time. Make it fun. Prepare a reward for meeting the goal. They will get there.

Slow and steady wins the race. Consider this beautiful example from ~Dorothy Canfield Fisher in her book, *Understood Betsy:*

"What's the matter?" asked the teacher, seeing her bewildered face.

"Why—why," said Elizabeth Ann, "I don't know what I am at all. If I'm second-grade arithmetic and seventh-grade reading and third-grade spelling, what grade am I?" The teacher laughed at the turn of her phrase. "You aren't any grade at all, no matter where you are in school. You're just yourself, aren't you? What difference does it make what grade you're in! And what's the use of your reading little baby things too easy for you just because you don't know your multiplication table?"

This time Elizabeth Ann didn't answer, because she herself didn't know what the matter was. But I do, and I'll tell you. The matter was that never before had she known what she was doing in school. She had always thought she was there to pass from one grade to another, and she was ever so startled to get a little glimpse of the fact that she was there to learn how to read and write and cipher and generally use her mind...

Don't let the curriculum be your master

It's quite common to feel that a school day (or school year) is not complete until a student has read every page of their textbook and filled in every line on the worksheets.

In most cases, you'll do those things without thinking about it. But there are times when the amount of work in a curriculum is excessive and unnecessary. This is called "busy work" and it should be utilized on a case-by-case basis.

For instance, if a child has shown that he has mastered long division, he may not need to work 30 problems a day. This can often cause burnout and frustration. Let him do 5-10 for review, and then move forward.

Drill is great. Excessive drill is not.

This applies to all other subjects. Use your discretion as the parent and the teacher. If a child is enjoying the work, there's no harm in letting them continue. As I mentioned in Chapter 2, some kids love worksheets! But if the concept has been thoroughly learned, and the child is feeling frustrated, don't waste his time or yours.

If you have a child who is great with the *content* of the lesson, but gets bogged down by writing, let them give you answers verbally. For many children, their comprehension skills are more advanced than their physical writing skills.

Let the curriculum be your guide, and not your master.

Trust your gut

Parents have instincts all the time, about every aspect of raising children. Without knowing why, we feel a strong conviction that something should be done a certain way.

That gut instinct is important in homeschooling. In Chapter 6 I talked a lot about parents who feel unqualified to educate their own children. I want you to remember that you know your child best, and you will make choices that are different from everyone else's. You'll do things that other people aren't doing. You'll choose a curriculum that works for your family. You'll have school on your own schedule.

If you are leaning toward a decision that doesn't seem normal, don't panic! Trust your gut. Homeschoolers are notorious for thinking outside the box.

Relationship is the most important part of homeschooling

In my twenty years of homeschooling, I've come to believe this more strongly every day. We are humans. We need relationships. We need to know we are loved and accepted.

As homeschooling parents, it's easy to get consumed by curriculum plans, schedules, and "getting it all done." While these all have their place, we need to remember that our relationships with our children are still number one.

Talk together about the things they are learning, even when they are old enough to be independent learners. Read aloud together whenever you can. Find time to do a hands-on project together.

Some days you will notice that school is not going smoothly. It could be that the math lesson is hard, or it could be that your child needs more of YOU than he needs of research papers today. Watch your children and pick up on these clues. Talk them through the difficult lessons, or even stop for the day and do something personal. Play a board game, go to the park, or make dinner together.

Build your relationships!

Long after your children graduate and move on to their adult lives, they will remember and cherish these personal times. Math lessons are necessary, but relationships are critical to humans.

Be the parent first, and the teacher second.

Conclusion

This book is the product of many discussions, both in real life and online, where frustrated and desperate parents expressed a desire to find an alternative to the public schools. Like so many, they automatically assumed that homeschooling was only for those families who had neatly organized lives, complete with a large income, a school room in their house, a college degree, and obedient children.

In one-on-one conversations I shared little snippets of the things in this book, and always added that, "Anyone can homeschool."

I hope and pray that you have found the inspiration, the encouragement, or the practical ideas you've been looking for. I hope now you realize that *anyone can homeschool*, and that you will tell others, too!

If you enjoyed Anyone Can Homeschool, I hope you will leave a review wherever you ordered your copy!

Remember to visit <u>AnyoneCanHomeschool.net</u> for lots of helpful links mentioned throughout this book.

Follow me on Facebook and Instagram!

Facebook.com/nickitruesdellblog

Instagram.com/nickitruesdell

Bibliography

Chapter 1:

1. Oklahoma, Univertisy of. 2017. *REQUIREMENTS FOR THE BACHELOR OF SCIENCE IN EDUCATION.* http://checksheets.ou.edu/16checksheets/element-2016.pdf.

2. University, Cleveland State. 2012. *Cleveland State University* https://www.csuohio.edu/undergradcatalog/edu/bsedu/mided.htm.

3. Hodson, Mariaemma Willis and Victoria Kindle. 1999. *Discover Your Child's Learning Style.* Crown Publishing.

Chapter 2:

4. https://vark-learn.com/introduction-to-vark/

5. https://vark-learn.com/introduction-to-vark/

6. Berquist, Laura. 2011. "Classical Education and How to Implement it in a Large Family." *Mother of Divine Grace School.* https://modg.org/curriculum/article/classical-education-and-how-to-implement-it-in-a-large-family.

7. White, Anne. n.d. "Introduction to Charlotte Mason." *Ambleside Online.* https://www.amblesideonline.org/WhatIsCM.shtml.

8. https://unitstudy.com/pages/what-is-a-unit-study

Chapter 4:

9. Bauer, Susan Wise. 2018. *Rethinking School.* New York: W. W. Norton & Company.

10. Bauer, Susan Wise. 2018. *Rethinking School*. New York: W. W. Norton & Company.

Chapter 6:

11. *Academic Performance of Homeschooled Students*; https://www.time4learning.com/homeschool/homeschoolstatistics.shtml#signif

Chapter 8:

12. Holzman, Sarita. 2018. *Sonlight blog*. April 18. https://blog.sonlight.com/how-to-boost-your-own-health-through-homeschooling.html?

13. Wayne, Israel; *Answers for Homeschooling*, Masterbooks 2018

Chapter 13

14. [1] Clarkson, Sally, *Seasons of a Mother's Heart*; Whole Heart Ministries, 1998